WHAT THE
RIVER
REVEALS

WHAT THE RIVER REVEALS

Understanding and Restoring Healthy Watersheds

Valerie Rapp

THE
MOUNTAINEERS

Published by
The Mountaineers
1001 SW Klickitat Way, Suite 201
Seattle, WA 98134

10 9 8 7
5 4 3 2 1

Published simultaneously in Great Britain by Cordee, 3a DeMontfort Street, Leicester, England, LE1 7HD

Manufactured in the United States of America

Edited by Mary Anne Stewart
Maps by Jerry Painter
Cover design by Amy Peppler Adams, designLab—Seattle
Book design and typography by Jennifer Shontz
Layout by Patrick Barber

Cover photograph: Santiam River, Oregon © Dennis Frates

Library of Congress Cataloging-in-Publication Data
Rapp, Valerie.
    What the river reveals : understanding and restoring healthy watersheds / Valerie Rapp.
        p.   cm.
    Includes bibliographical references and index.
    ISBN 0-89886-527-1
    1. Stream ecology—Northwest, Pacific. 2. Stream conservation—Northwest, Pacific. 3. Rivers—Northwest, Pacific. I. Title.
QH104.5.N6R36 1997
577.6'4'09795—dc21   97-27607
                                                              CIP

 Printed on recycled paper

Permissions

To Gene

The river of marriage is made of many streams: romantic love, friendship, loyalties, shared memories, a common language and also silence, giving and receiving on many levels. The river of marriage is made of the substance of life itself.

Love, Val

Contents

Maps

Figure

Table

Acknowledgments

MANY PEOPLE SHARED THEIR KNOWLEDGE and personal insights with me as I learned about river issues and river ecology. My job as a writer was to interpret scientific and historical information in a way interesting to the general reader while keeping it scientifically accurate. Any mistakes are my own.

Many employees of state and federal agencies shared their time and thoughts with me freely. These men and women offered their knowledge, professional enthusiasm, and thoughtful opinions. Almost without exception, however, they told me that they had been advised not to talk with the press and asked me not to use their names in my book. I thank each one who shared his or her time with me—you know who you are. The U.S. Forest Service, National Marine Fisheries Service, U.S. Fish and Wildlife Service, Washington Department of Fisheries, Oregon Department of Fish and Wildlife, and Oregon Department of Forestry should be proud to have such intelligent, dedicated employees.

The Springfield Library reference librarians were especially helpful in obtaining many difficult-to-find references from libraries around the Pacific Northwest and were always professional and courteous.

Many scientists and consultants made the time for me to interview them at length and often shared publications and research results with me. I am grateful for their time and expertise. My appreciation goes to Charley Dewberry and Chris Frissell for the Pacific Rivers Council workshops; to Stan Gregory for including me in the H.J. Andrews flood pulse workshop; to Gordon Reeves, Jim Lichatowich, Willa Nehlsen, and Jim Karr for taking the time to meet with me; to Jim Martin for an excellent presentation. I also thank Chris Frissell for sharing his map of fish decline and extinction in the Pacific Northwest and California; Pete Lawson for sharing his graph on ocean cycles, freshwater habitat, and the decline of salmon; Sheri Schneider and Sara Freedman of the Natural Resources Conservation Service for providing me with a copy of their agency's map of Oregon floodplain areas; and Northwest Environmental Advocates for developing their maps on sources of water pollution in the Columbia and

Willamette Rivers. I depended on maps from the U.S. Forest Service for my map of existing and proposed key watersheds on federal lands; maps from the Bonneville Power Administration and Northwest Power Planning Council for my map of dams and salmon habitat in the Columbia River basin; and maps from the Lower Columbia River Bi-State Water Quality Program for sources of water pollution in the lower Columbia River.

This book would never have existed without the support, encouragement, and hard work of the staff of The Mountaineers Books. I am very grateful to Margaret Foster and Donna DeShazo for their support and encouragement, and also wish to thank Uma Kukathas and everyone on the editorial, production, and marketing staff for their help. I appreciate very much Mary Anne Stewart's thorough and insightful editing.

My warmest thanks go to my family, for believing in me as a writer. My parents, Harry and Teresa Rapp, have been enthusiastic about my writing since I penciled my first stories at six years old, and my in-laws, Gene and Eva Skrine, have offered continued interest and encouragement. I am grateful to my stepchildren, Adam, Leah, and Sarah Skrine, for their good humor and support, and for the special joy they have brought into my life; special thanks to Leah for her idea about the prologue. I especially want to thank my husband, Gene Skrine, who accompanied me on field trips, took photographs, read rough drafts, provided comfort on bad writing days, handled household chores while I worked to meet my deadline, and believed in the book and in me. We share life on many levels.

Prologue: The Floods of 1996

EVERY FALL IN THE PACIFIC NORTHWEST, we wait for the winter rains to come. September and early October rains are just passing showers. Sometime in late October or November, though, storms sweep in off the Pacific Ocean that are unmistakably a change of season, and everyone knows the winter rains are here. The wind knocks the gold and yellow leaves from the bigleaf maples and cottonwoods, branches snap off the Douglas-firs, and a dampness settles in that will last until spring. It's so wet that even mushrooms rot. Rivers rise.

The winter of 1996 started in the fall of 1995, when the winter rains arrived in November. Storm after storm rolled ashore like waves off the ocean, sweeping across parts of Oregon, Washington, Idaho, and Montana. Rain-saturated soils on steep mountain slopes gave way, rivers rose to the top of their banks, and a few poured over. It was the third wettest November on record in Portland, Oregon. It was also the warmest November on record, so even at high elevations in the mountains it was raining instead of snowing.

In December, hurricane-force winds blew over the Oregon coast, through the Willamette Valley, and over southwest Washington. Gusts of over 119 miles per hour were recorded at Sea Lion Caves, north of the Siuslaw River on the Oregon coast. Where winds were the strongest, on ridge tops and along valley corridors, some trees snapped, and others tore out by the roots. The last half of December was dry.

In the Pacific Northwest, the depth of the winter snowpack in the mountains indicates what the next summer's water supply will be like: how much water will fill the reservoirs, how much farmers can pump for irrigation, and how much cities will have for their people. On January 1, 1996, the snowpack in the Cascades was well below average.

January started out warm, and heavy rainfall melted some of the little snow there was at high elevations. But halfway through January the weather turned cold, and it snowed all the way from the mountaintops to the valleys, with heavy snow in the high country day after day. Willamette Pass got 203 inches of snow in fourteen days—almost

seventeen feet. In mid-January, the snowpack in the Oregon C
was only 29 percent of average for the time of year. Just two week
on January 31, it had deepened to 112 percent of average—a wi
worth of snow in two weeks.

The late January cold snap froze the ground underneath all the s
in western Oregon and western Washington, and in early February,
ice storm spread a layer of ice on top of the snow in the Willamette Vai
ley. Then came one of the sudden weather reverses so common in the
winter of 1996. A front nicknamed the "Pineapple Express" blew out of
the South Pacific Ocean and across the Pacific Northwest. Its surge of
subtropical moisture brought heavy rain and sent temperatures up into
the fifties and even sixties. The intense storm lasted from February 6 to
February 8 across western Oregon and western Washington. Eugene got
5.17 inches of rain in one twenty-four-hour period. Cells of torrential rain
were embedded within the front, and some areas were drenched with
much worse rainfall than Eugene. Laurel Mountain, in the Oregon Coast
Range, caught 8.2 inches of rain in twenty-four hours, and more than
23 inches in three days.

Normally the soils of western Oregon and Washington can absorb
enormous amounts of water, but the Pineapple Express dropped warm
rain on deep snow that lay on top of frozen ground. As much as 12 inches
of snow melted and added to the water running off the slowly thawing
ground. The frozen soil finally thawed, but the ground's natural capacity to transport water was quickly exceeded. Rivers overflowed their
banks, and the earth moved.

The flood of '96 rolled over the landscape at the speed of the rising
rivers. For people who lived in the upper ends of watersheds, the flood
came quickly with little warning that this time would be different from
the high waters they expected every winter. The Mohawk River, a
tributary of the McKenzie, crested at an estimated 22.2 feet, 7 feet
over flood stage and the highest level ever recorded on the river. In
northwest Oregon, the Nehalem River crested at 27.4 feet, over 13 feet
above flood stage.

People who lived downstream on the Willamette and Columbia Rivers had one or two days' warning as the flood rolled toward them. The
Willamette reclaimed much of its old floodplain in the Willamette Valley, spreading out over fields, roads, and homes and stretching one or two
miles wide in some places. On Friday, February 9, two days after the
McKenzie River peaked, the lower Willamette crested in Portland more
than 10 feet above flood stage. It carried broken pieces of houses, sheds,

docks, boats, and other debris in its swirling waters. Below Portland, the flood moved steadily down the Columbia, cresting at Vancouver, Washington, at 6:00 P.M. on Friday and downriver at the Oregon town of Saint Helens at midnight Friday, finally flowing into the Pacific Ocean sometime on Saturday.

Eight people died in Oregon, including an eight-year-old girl who stepped off her driveway into an overflowing ditch and was washed into a culvert, and a sixty-two-year-old woman whose home was swept into the Sandy River by a mudslide. An estimated twenty-two thousand people had to evacuate their homes, including all twelve thousand residents of Keizer, a town near Salem.

Twenty-six rivers reached or exceeded flood stage, as measured by water-gauging stations. Hundreds of smaller rivers and streams also flooded. Mudslides, floodwaters, or sinkholes blocked most major highways around the state. Rivers flowed into hundreds of houses and down the streets of several towns, including Keizer, Tillamook, Oregon City, and Lake Oswego. In the Tillamook area of northwest Oregon, hundreds of dairy cows drowned or broke their legs struggling in flooded barns. Millions of gallons of untreated sewage poured into rivers as sewage treatment plants were inundated. The Pacific Rivers Council contracted Pacific Watershed Associates to do an aerial reconnaissance of landslides in the mountains. In nine hours of flying, the observers spotted roughly five hundred landslides in the Oregon Coast Range and Cascades.

By March, river levels had returned to normal, their muddy waters had cleared up, the grass had turned green, and willows were budding. People tore out their ruined walls and floors and started to rebuild. Everyone talked about the flood of '96 in the past tense.

Then the winter rains returned in November of 1996. Another Pineapple Express rolled in—a tropical storm heavy with moisture. From November 17 through 19, it rained relentlessly. In most places it didn't pour quite as hard as the previous February, and there was little snowpack to melt since it was early in the winter, but it rained more than enough to flood again. The local TV newscasters used the same "Flood of '96" logos they had developed six months earlier, and for the second time in a year, floods and landslides reworked the landscape of the Pacific Northwest.

The heaviest rains hit, generally, at different spots than the first flood, except for the Mohawk River, which was struck hard both times. South of Eugene, the Coast Fork of the Willamette flooded, and west of Eugene the Siuslaw poured over its banks. But the dramatic center of the

A logjam on the McKenzie River acts like a catcher's mitt, catching driftwood carried downstream during the November 1996 flood. (Val Rapp)

November 1996 flood was the Umpqua River in southern Oregon.

The Umpqua begins in the Cascades and cuts through the Oregon Coast Range to the ocean. Highway 38 follows the river valley through part of the Coast Range. The mountains along this stretch of the river have a naturally high rate of landslides because the underlying geology is unstable, the slopes are steep, the soil is thin, and rock outcroppings are frequent. Much of the area is privately owned timberlands, and much of it has been logged. The Pineapple Express of November 1996 dumped its heaviest rainfall on this vulnerable landscape, and the mountains moved. A total of 137 landslides crashed down on Highway 38 along the roughly 60-mile stretch between Interstate 5 and the coast, trapping seventy motorists and residents between slides. One driver was killed when the mud and rocks crushed her car and pushed it into the river. A truck trying to stop in mudslide debris hit another car, shoving it into the current below. The husband escaped, but his wife and two children were pinned in the car and died.

On November 18, 1996, about twenty miles south of Highway 38, a landslide began on Rock Creek, a tributary of the Umpqua. The debris flow started in a 168-acre clear-cut high on a mountain slope, with shallow and rocky soils and an 80 percent grade. The harvest unit had been logged in 1987 by Champion International, the landowner at the time, and replanted in compliance with all Oregon forest practices regulations. Head-high Douglas-firs were growing there when the storm hit. The rain-saturated soils gave way, and the mass of mud and water poured down Rock Creek. It scoured the stream channel through forty acres of old-growth forest on federal forest lands below the clear-cut, picking up trees, boulders, and mud on its way.

The debris flow came out of the forest, hit the house belonging to the Moon family, wiped it out, and slid on down Rock Creek to the bottom of the slope. Four people were killed: Rick and Susan Moon, husband and wife, and neighbor Sharon Marvin—all in the Moons' house when the slide struck—and friend Ann Maxwell, who was walking up the road to the house. The Moons' two children survived.

Heavy storms continued through the rest of November and December, leading to record-breaking annual rainfalls for most western Oregon cities. Eugene had 77.17 inches of rain, compared with its thirty-year average of 49.37 inches. Yet another storm from the South Pacific hit the West at the end of December, with the heaviest rainfall centered south of Oregon, causing floods and more deaths in southern Oregon, central California, and Nevada.

The floodwaters were still receding when the rising tide of commentary began. Some people charged that we had caused the disasters ourselves, with the intensive logging of the last thirty years. Others claimed that dams and levees we had built had kept the floods from being even more damaging. Longtime residents pointed out that the Christmas flood of 1964 had been just as bad and that some areas where houses now stood used to flood regularly years ago: it was people's own fault that they had moved onto floodplains that belonged to the rivers. A few said it was the Pacific Northwest's growing cities that had caused the floods: the region had too many people—and some of the others should leave.

What have we done to our rivers?

What the River Reveals explores the health and ecology of Pacific Northwest rivers. What makes a river healthy? How are a river and its watershed connected? What is the condition of our Pacific Northwest rivers? How can we restore our rivers and keep them healthy? These questions are at the heart of this book. The answers will give us a better understanding of the floods of 1996, and of rivers in general.

Chapter 1, "Going Upriver," presents an overview of the rivers of the Pacific Northwest and basic ideas about river health. Chapter 2, "The Elegant Connection," and Chapter 3, "Disturbance and Resilience," explore the ecology of healthy rivers. Chapter 4, "Respect and Transformation," narrates the history of the people and rivers of the Pacific Northwest, from four thousand years ago to the beginning of the twentieth century. Chapter 5, "Broken Connections"; Chapter 6, "The Simplified Landscape"; Chapter 7, "Uncoupling an Ecosystem"; and Chapter 8, "The Landscape of Salmon," examine how we have changed our rivers in the twentieth century. Chapter 9, "Restoration," suggests some principles and approaches for river restoration. In Chapter 10, "Refuge," I take a final look at the questions raised in this book, and in the "Bibliographic Notes," I briefly discuss some of the most important sources I used in my research.

Pacific Northwest rivers have natural resources and beauty that are the envy of the rest of the country. They are famous for white water, scenic beauty, and high water quality, and wild salmon still return to many of them. However, these rivers have also been greatly changed by human activities over the last two hundred years—by dams and other water development projects, and by logging, farming, and urban and industrial development.

There is a feeling throughout the Pacific Northwest (and for good reason) that our rivers have reached a critical point. In *What the River Reveals,* I hope to help readers understand why Pacific Northwest rivers are on the edge, and what they need to be healthy again.

Source of map, pages 18 and 19: Based on map from *Columbia–North Pacific Region Comprehensive Framework Study of Water and Related Lands,* by Pacific Northwest River Basins Commission, 1969.

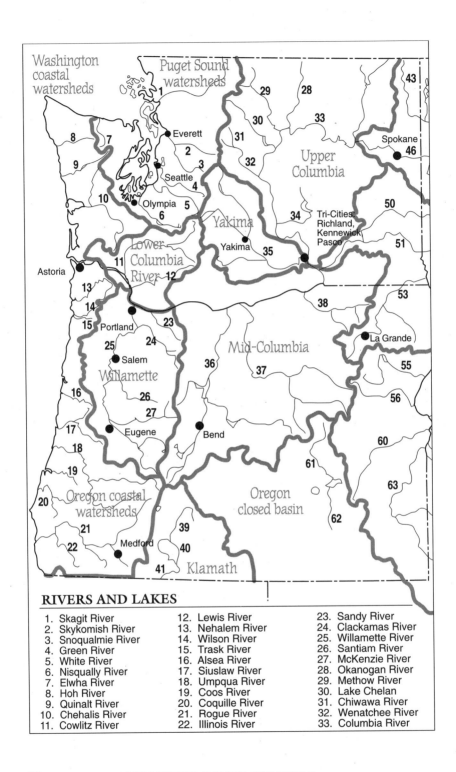

RIVERS AND LAKES

1. Skagit River	12. Lewis River	23. Sandy River
2. Skykomish River	13. Nehalem River	24. Clackamas River
3. Snoqualmie River	14. Wilson River	25. Willamette River
4. Green River	15. Trask River	26. Santiam River
5. White River	16. Alsea River	27. McKenzie River
6. Nisqually River	17. Siuslaw River	28. Okanogan River
7. Elwha River	18. Umpqua River	29. Methow River
8. Hoh River	19. Coos River	30. Lake Chelan
9. Quinalt River	20. Coquille River	31. Chiwawa River
10. Chehalis River	21. Rogue River	32. Wenatchee River
11. Cowlitz River	22. Illinois River	33. Columbia River

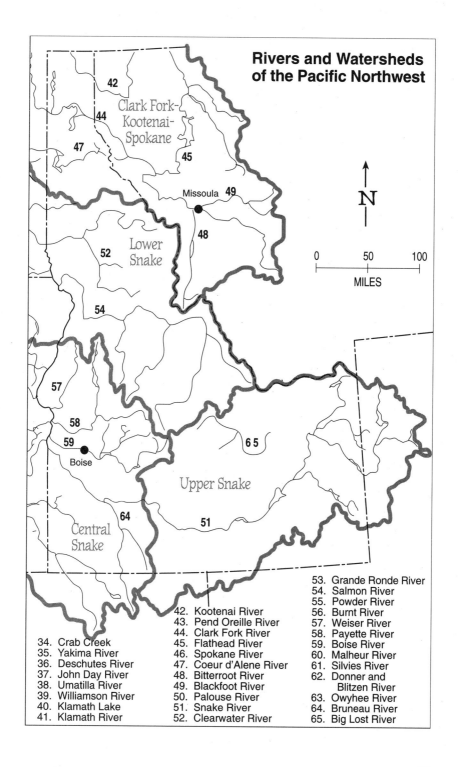

Rivers and Watersheds of the Pacific Northwest

42

Clark Fork-
Kootenai-
Spokane

44

47

45

Missoula 49

48

N

0   50   100

MILES

52   Lower
Snake

54

57

58

59

Boise

6 5

Upper Snake

64

51

Central
Snake

34. Crab Creek
35. Yakima River
36. Deschutes River
37. John Day River
38. Umatilla River
39. Williamson River
40. Klamath Lake
41. Klamath River

42. Kootenai River
43. Pend Oreille River
44. Clark Fork River
45. Flathead River
46. Spokane River
47. Coeur d'Alene River
48. Bitterroot River
49. Blackfoot River
50. Palouse River
51. Snake River
52. Clearwater River

53. Grande Ronde River
54. Salmon River
55. Powder River
56. Burnt River
57. Weiser River
58. Payette River
59. Boise River
60. Malheur River
61. Silvies River
62. Donner and
    Blitzen River
63. Owyhee River
64. Bruneau River
65. Big Lost River

Chapter 1

Going Upriver

I'm driving home from town on a beautiful spring day. I've just spent two days on the Oregon coast at a workshop sponsored by Pacific Rivers Council, an environmental group. We waded up streams and climbed over logs while Charley Dewberry, the council's stream restoration coordinator, talked to us about stream restoration and stream health in the Pacific Northwest. I took as many notes as I could, jotting down snippets of conversation while standing calf-deep in the water, at lunch eating a sandwich with one hand and writing with the other. Charley kept moving and talking. He stopped occasionally to sip from his jug of orange juice, but not for long because he had so much he wanted to share with the group. We were soil scientists, fish biologists, foresters, and one writer—me. On the road home, I'm thinking about what Charley said.

"How do we know what a healthy river looks like?" Charley asked. "How do we diagnose the health of an ecosystem?"

He answered his own question:

You have to develop a skill for it, the way a doctor develops a skill for diagnosing a person's health. Some people have gone away from these workshops frustrated because they wanted me to give them a set of prescriptions. But you can't learn a skill that way. It's like learning to ride a bicycle. I can't teach you how to do it by giving you a set of equations about the physics of what happens when you ride a bicycle. You have to learn the skill by doing it.

The rivers people have at home are all different. All I can do is help them build the ability to diagnose the health of the river.

They'll have to study their own river at home and figure out what its condition is, and what they can do to make it healthy again.

My home is up the McKenzie River Highway, fifty miles east of the cities of Eugene and Springfield in western Oregon. I'm still looping around Springfield on the freeway. I drive past the fast-growing Gateway area, with its mall, office buildings, and apartment complexes. Sony is building a plant that will make compact discs, both the musical and the computer kinds. A little farther on, the Weyerhaeuser mill sprawls across the landscape. The big log decks and the white plumes of steam and smoke are good signs—the mill is still operating, still providing jobs. These are the signs of a healthy economy. But what does a healthy river look like?

To my left, on the far side of the freeway from the mill, the McKenzie River meanders quietly through cottonwoods and alders, with riffles where it curves around a small island. Patches of grass and blackberries break up the wooded areas. The clear, sparkling water is set off by the fresh spring greens of the cottonwood leaves and grass. Is the McKenzie a healthy river? The scene I'm driving by is beautiful and inviting. If this isn't a healthy river, then what's wrong?

Charley suggested that one step to assessing a river's health is to find out what the river was like historically, when European-Americans first came to the Pacific Northwest. What did the river and its valley look like, how much water flowed in the river, what kinds of fish lived there, and how many fish? He suggested that we dig into the files of historical societies and county courthouses. We should read original survey records and the journals of Lewis and Clark, trappers, and early settlers.

Charley did this kind of research on the Siuslaw, the river on the central Oregon coast where he's been working for the last several years. He found a journal left by Alexander McLeod, a Hudson's Bay Company trapper who visited the Siuslaw in 1826. When McLeod headed upriver in a canoe, he found a logjam more than one mile long that extended across the entire valley from foothill to foothill. Over time, perhaps centuries, thousands of trees and parts of trees had toppled into the river and been swept into the massive pile by periodic floods. The jam was so huge that floods could rework only parts of it, never destroy it. The river channel was braided and complex, and the entire valley floor was part of the floodplain.

The Siuslaw River valley looks a lot different now. The big logjams are gone and so are the old-growth cedars, Sitka spruce, and Douglas-firs that provided the material for them. The valley today has pastures interspersed with houses and gardens. The river flows in a single, downcut channel, with a thin strip of alder trees along the bank. It takes a major flood for the Siuslaw to rise to the top of its banks. An occasional log or stump lies stranded on the tidal flats, half buried in mud.

Physical appearance isn't the only thing that has changed for the Siuslaw. During the late 1800s, the river's coho salmon run averaged 218,000 fish each year. To put that number in perspective, Charley pointed out that the 1993 escapement goal for coho salmon from Cape Falcon (about thirty-five miles south of the Columbia River) to the Mexican border was just 68,000 fish (escapement is the number of salmon that return to a river and succeed in spawning). But not even that modest number of coho returned. "So at the turn of the century," Charley said, "the Siuslaw River alone supported a fishery four times larger than the largest recent California and Oregon coast fishery south of Cape Falcon." During the early 1990s, an average of 2,500 coho were coming back each year to the Siuslaw—about 1 percent of the original run.

Charley suggested that we could measure the health of our rivers by the salmon. By this yardstick, the Siuslaw River of the 1800s, with its logjams, big trees, and multiple channels, was healthy, and the crashing coho runs of the 1990s tell us that the river is now seriously ill. We are at this workshop to begin learning how to diagnose rivers. The fact that foresters and soil scientists are here with fish biologists shows that we are beginning to recognize that there are links between trees, dirt, and healthy rivers.

The freeway ends on the east edge of Springfield. I turn left on the McKenzie River Highway. It goes east through several miles of suburban edge, cuts along the toe of the foothills, then begins its journey up the valley. The highway and the river are the two continuous lines that connect the entire McKenzie River valley. One is a ribbon of asphalt, hard and unyielding, laid on the surface of the landscape by machinery. The other is a ribbon of flowing water, abiding but not unchanging, and it permeates the entire landscape, carrying the story of the valley in its waters.

The McKenzie Valley is wide here, with filbert orchards, blueberry farms, peppermint fields, and cattle pastures. The older houses are modest bungalows or farmhouses, likely to be owned by a filbert farmer, a log truck driver, or a waitress at the Lucky Logger restaurant. Mixed among the older homes are splashy new houses with multiple levels and elaborate decks that overlook either the river or the valley. These new homes are apt to belong to well-off retirees, or to professionals who commute to town.

It's late April, and the valley is like a fairyland. The rhododendrons and azaleas are at their peak. These rain-loving bushes are quintessentially Pacific Northwest. Their dark green, glossy leaves and masses of large, open-throated flowers—cascades of pink, red, white, orange, and purple—make a showy display in almost every yard along the highway. Dogwoods, apple trees, lilacs, and wild irises are also blooming.

The foothills are covered with a mosaic of second-growth Douglas-fir forests. The slopes are all green, but the shades and textures vary from hillside to hillside. Maturing forests are dark green, seventy to a hundred or more feet tall and rough textured. Young clear-cuts are light green, the grasses and ferns not yet dominated by the growing trees. Scattered patches of a light greenish-brown are the newest clear-cuts, the grass and trees not yet grown enough to completely cover the logging slash.

The hillside reminds me of another point made by Charley. Someone asked what authorities or references we could turn to for more information. Charley answered that Hippocrates was one of the best

Historical photos offer clues to how rivers have changed since the 1800s. In the 1920s, forests along the upper McKenzie River were mostly intact. (photo courtesy Lane County Historical Museum, M1G/L78-551Q. Smith Mountjoy Collection)

guides on the subject of river restoration. Hippocrates emphasized treating the whole person, not just the sick organ, and was the first physician to look at how the environment affected a person's health. According to Charley, "In stream restoration, we are now at the point where Hippocrates and the other ancient Greeks were with medicine two thousand years ago."

A good doctor, Charley told us, diagnoses an illness by looking at the whole person, not just at the blood, or the liver, or the spleen. He wanted to practice medicine the same way Hippocrates did—Charley wanted to cure his patients by treating the whole system, not just the sick organ— only Charley wanted to be a doctor for rivers.

You can't diagnose the health of a river through a narrow focus on the river itself, Charley emphasized. You have to look at the watershed that the river flows through. To diagnose the health of the McKenzie River, then, I must look at all of this, too—the forest mosaic of the foothills, the new houses, the peppermint fields. To look at the health of Pacific Northwest rivers, I need to look at our entire Pacific Northwest landscape. Rivers are embedded in their watersheds.

WATERSHEDS OF THE PACIFIC NORTHWEST

I can describe a watershed in two different ways, depending on which definition I use. To scientists, a watershed is the ridgeline that defines the boundaries of the river basin. We use this meaning figuratively when we call something a "watershed event." Raindrops falling on one side of the ridgeline eventually run downhill into one river, while raindrops falling on the other side flow into a different river.

Under its other definition, the one generally used by people who are not scientists, a watershed is the basin defined by the ridgelines. The watershed, or catchment, is the entire area drained by a specific river or stream. And just as ecosystems can be at many scales, so can watersheds. Within the McKenzie watershed, there is the Sweetwater Creek watershed, the French Pete Creek watershed, and many others. The McKenzie, on the other hand, is just a small part of the larger Columbia River watershed.

We tend to experience the landscape as linear. We know our way around by roads and highways. We divide our landscape with lines that demarcate counties, states, countries. Topographical maps overlay the natural contours of the land with a surveyor's grid of township, range, and section lines, dividing the Pacific Northwest into square-mile sections. But water experiences the landscape as shape. If we try to see the Pacific Northwest the way a raindrop sees it—as shape—we see the contours that create watersheds. If we look at watersheds, we see a different map.

From this perspective, we see a giant, many-fingered watershed consuming all of the Pacific Northwest except for the Coast Ranges, Puget Sound, and southeastern Oregon. This sprawling, amorphous beast is the Columbia River basin. It includes parts of seven states and two Canadian provinces. The Columbia River drains an area of about 258,000 square miles, a watershed larger than France and including roughly 75 percent of the states of Washington, Oregon, and Idaho. Its annual average stream flow is more than ten times the flow of the Colorado River. When the twelve-hundred-mile-long Columbia finally reaches the ocean, it pours its waters into the Pacific from a mouth five miles wide at a rate of 2 million gallons a second.

The Columbia River basin is composed of irregularly shaped wedges and ovals that are the tributary basins of this megawatershed: the Snake, Salmon, Kootenai, Wenatchee, Yakima, John Day, Deschutes, and Willamette Rivers, among others. At its top, the basin has a long, sharp point that juts into Canada. On the southeast, the Snake River watershed makes a large bulge. The McKenzie River watershed is a relatively small wedge of 1,300 square miles on the west side of the Oregon Cascades, roughly halfway between the Columbia River and the California border.

Around the edges of the Columbia River basin, other watersheds drain the rest of the Pacific Northwest. The Coast Ranges of Oregon and Washington have many small watersheds that plunge directly into the Pacific Ocean. Where Puget Sound reaches into Washington like a watery hand reaching into a bucket of mountains, rivers flow into the sound from the east, south, and west. In southwestern Oregon, the Umpqua and Rogue Rivers begin in the Cascades and cut across the Coast Range to the ocean, the only Pacific Northwest rivers other than the Columbia to cut across both these ranges. In south-central Oregon, the Klamath Basin drains the southern end of the Oregon Cascades and then flows south into California. A small part of southeastern Idaho is part of the Great Basin. Finally, a large part of southeastern Oregon forms the Oregon closed basin, with the few rivers that cross the sagebrush desert flowing into large, shallow, mostly alkaline lakes and never reaching the ocean. Each watershed catches all the rain and snow that fall within its boundaries, cradles the water within the ridges and folds of its landscape, and funnels it down to the river. Water shaping itself to the land connects the entire watershed.

Think about just the McKenzie watershed for a minute, because it's too hard to think about the entire Columbia River basin at once. Visualize the McKenzie as a great, three-sided, wedge-shaped basin. The basin is tilted, over ten thousand feet high at its wide end along the Cascade peaks and less than four hundred feet high at its tapered end, where the water pours out into the Willamette River. Imagine this three-sided basin now wrinkling and corrugating into a highly complex landscape. The major corrugations are the major drainages: the mainstem, South Fork, and East Fork of the McKenzie; the Blue River; and the Mohawk River. Within each of these major drainages are a thousand wrinkles—mountains, ridges, canyons, streams. The landscape has glaciers, lava flows, old-growth forests, clear-cuts, farms, towns, and mills. It's full of life, from the calypso orchids blooming along the riverbank to the spotted owl hunting a forested ridge, to the chinook salmon fry drifting downriver toward the ocean, to the river rafter and store clerk. The McKenzie River is the thread that connects the entire landscape. Inevitably, inescapably, whatever happens in the watershed is reflected in the river.

The water flowing through the watershed makes the connections. Raindrops splash on tree branches, fall to the ground, and soak into the earth. Snow falls on the mountainsides, piles up in deep drifts, and melts in the spring. Water moves underground, between grains of dirt, through cracks and passages in the lava flows, through porous layers of rock. Springs bubble up in small hollows lush with lady ferns and mosses. Snowmelt trickles down steep draws, and small streams splash over fallen logs in deep canyons. Smaller streams run into bigger streams, which join into yet bigger ones that flow into rivers. A diagram of the McKenzie's stream network would look something like our circulatory system—a finely branched network in which the many tiny capillaries run into bigger and bigger blood vessels. The stream network, of course, would not be as symmetrical; it would be full of hooks, curves, and unexpected bends. And whereas each person's network of blood vessels is contained within an individual body, the McKenzie merges into the Willamette, the Willamette flows into the Columbia, and the Columbia pours the mingled water of hundreds of rivers into the ocean.

As the water moves through the basin, it affects its surroundings and is also affected by them. If the soil is bare, the rain erodes dirt off the hillside. A stream scours a pool where it plunges over a large fallen tree. Rain falling on a filbert orchard dissolves fertilizer and washes some of the nitrogen and phosphorus into the river, affecting its chemical balance

The curves of old channels are still visible on the Willamette River floodplain. The river is now restricted to a single channel in most places. (photo courtesty Oregon Historical Society, OrHi 55547)

and its food web. Whatever nature or humans do in a watershed, it is ultimately revealed in the river. If the watershed is healthy, the river is healthy. And, of course, if the watershed is not healthy, its degradation shows in the river.

THE SHAPE OF WILD RIVERS

In the Pacific Northwest we have looked at our rivers as raw material to be shaped to our desires. When European-Americans explored them in the 1800s, the rivers were wild and awesome, full of rapids, waterfalls, cascades, and chutes. The mountains held so many waterfalls that the region's major range—the Cascades—is named after them. When Lewis and Clark boated down the Columbia in October 1805, through the Narrows stretch in the Cascades, they described the river as "this agitated gut swelling, boiling & whorling in every direction."

In the valleys, large rivers like the Willamette had multiple channels that twisted and braided across a wide floodplain congested with logjams, wetlands, sloughs, and islands. In 1854, the multiple channels of the Willamette created a river complex two to three miles wide. Although most of the Willamette Valley was prairie or (by then) farmland, thick forest grew between the river channels, extending out for half a mile on both sides of the banks. Thousands of trees had fallen into the river and were piled up in logjams, mired in the bottom, or stuck in side channels.

Floods pulsed down the rivers during heavy winter rains or during spring runoff, when the mountain snows melted. The freshets poured out across the broad floodplains and rearranged the whole tangled mess of channels and logs and islands. The Pacific Northwest rivers of the early 1800s wrestled with the wild landscape as equals.

But wild rivers were not what we wanted. We wanted something more useful—something more controlled. We wanted to grow wheat and corn and peppermint on the rich soils of the floodplains, to ship wheat and lumber down the river in barges, to generate electricity with the water tumbling down from the mountains, to build cities on the riverbanks and floodplains. We cleared the logjams, squeezed the rivers into single channels, drained wetlands, and diverted water into irrigation canals. By the 1960s, the Willamette River was confined to a single channel bordered by a narrow line of trees, with occasional islands and some outlying ponds surviving as remnants of other channels. But we did not really get the control we wanted until we checked the rivers with dams.

Today in the Pacific Northwest, almost every river of any size has at least one dam on it, and most rivers are stoppered with a series of barriers built on their tributaries and mainstems. The dams are clustered near the mountain ranges, where dropping elevations create the head needed for generating electricity and where canyons hold deep reservoirs. During the winter rains and spring runoff, the dams prevent floods by holding water back. Year-round, they replace the natural peaks and drops of seasonal water flow with an artificial cycle built around fluctuating demands for electricity. Behind the dams, reservoirs drown the rapids and cascades of wild rivers under quiet lakes.

Rivers that once fit into the landscape and the seasons are now engineered to fit our society. Almost every stream and river in the Pacific Northwest has been changed radically since the arrival of European-Americans in the early 1800s. Only a few among us—Native Americans, fishermen, fish biologists—asked how these changes were affecting the health of rivers. When salmon runs began to drop, we responded to the dilemma as an engineering problem, not as a river health problem. We attempted to fix it by building fish hatcheries and fish ladders and by developing new fishing regulations. Until a few years ago, the question of river health was generally ignored.

CONNECTIONS

I'm over forty miles east of Springfield now, driving up the McKenzie River Highway, just a short way from home, and I'm passing the turn-off for the H.J. Andrews Experimental Forest, which is part of the Willamette National Forest. The experimental forest is well off the highway and little noticed by people in Blue River besides Forest Service employees, but it is famous among forest scientists and stream ecologists. Many of the newest ideas and best science on old-growth forests, forest ecosystems, streams, and watersheds have come from research done on the Andrews and neighboring areas in the McKenzie watershed. Scientists and researchers have come and gone for years, unnoticed by the community. Research on forests progresses about as fast as a tree grows and is about as exciting to watch. No one paid attention for twenty or thirty years while researchers like Jerry Franklin, Fred Swanson, and Stan Gregory slowly accumulated data.

In the 1980s, researchers began to emerge with new information about old-growth forests. For years, foresters had been taught that old-growth forests were biological deserts, decadent stands to be cut and replaced with faster-growing younger trees. In fact, scientists now said, the old-growth forest was an incredibly complex ecosystem with tremendous biodiversity, albeit the diversity was found in such forms as fungi, spiders, and bats. That diversity might not seem important (who needs a mycorrhizal fungus the size of a marble?), but researchers had also discovered that many of these obscure species played key roles in the ecosystem, and without them the conifer forests, whether old-growth or second-growth, would eventually decline, possibly even collapse.

The war in the Pacific Northwest over forests, owls, timber, and salmon was already fierce. People on all sides of the issue used the new information in their own way. Some claimed the research showed that old-growth forests were irreplaceable treasures and should all be set aside as reserves. Others insisted we could use the new information to manage the forests differently, in order to have both healthy forests and logging. By the late 1980s, the scientists and their information were suddenly important. The Andrews got money to replace its ramshackle collection of rusting trailers with a set of buildings that actually looked like a research station. The researchers were swamped with requests to speak at conferences and to testify in court as expert witnesses. In 1993, the year of President Clinton's Forest Conference, Oregon governor Barbara Roberts and Secretary of the Interior Bruce Babbitt came to tour the Andrews and to listen to what the researchers had to say.

The scientists of the Andrews were also developing new ideas about streams, but their theories were little noticed during the 1980s, when legal and political battles were being fought over forests and land. It was not until the 1990s, when the public's attention turned to salmon, that a wider public began to learn about these new concepts.

The salmon runs of the Pacific Northwest once numbered in the tens of millions. Coho, pink, chum, sockeye, chinook: five species of salmon—hundreds of individual runs—returned from the ocean each year, swimming up every river and stream of the finely webbed network that spread across the Pacific Northwest. Strong and supple after their adventurous lives in the open ocean, these salmon migrated hundreds of miles upstream, deep into Idaho and British Columbia as well as Oregon and Washington. They muscled their way up rapids where a man couldn't even stand in the current. They jumped up and over plunging, crashing waterfalls like Celilo and Willamette. The big chinook that came back to the uppermost reaches of the Columbia River were known as June hogs because they weighed over a hundred pounds each. Most Native American cultures in the Pacific Northwest were built around the salmon as food and myth, and as emblem of the relationship between humans and nature.

Salmon runs have been declining and disappearing ever since European-Americans began to settle the Pacific Northwest, but their numbers plunged dramatically during the 1980s. The Columbia River system alone once had 10 to 16 million salmon returning to spawn annually. By the early 1990s, only about 1.1 million salmon entered the river each year, and 75 percent of those were hatchery fish. That left the wild salmon of the Columbia at just 1 to 5 percent of their historic numbers and dropping. In 1991 and 1992, in response to petitions from environmentalists, the National Marine Fisheries Service listed Snake River sockeye salmon as an endangered species and Snake River spring/summer and fall chinook as threatened species. Environmental groups immediately began to petition for the listing of more salmon runs, and the plummeting populations in many rivers made it seem likely that the petitions would be successful.

The Endangered Species Act required the federal government to provide recovery plans for the listed salmon runs. Salmon need cold, clean water, and they need suitable habitat in rivers and streams for the freshwater part of their life cycles. In short, they need healthy rivers. Because you can have a healthy river only if you have a healthy watershed, any recovery plans for salmon would have to deal with the whole watershed.

And practically all watersheds in the Pacific Northwest were salmon watersheds.

Suddenly, old-growth forests and spotted owls began to look like almost a small issue. The cost of protecting and restoring salmon runs would be enormous, many times the cost of protecting old-growth forests in reserves. Salmon recovery would require changes in the way the hydro-electric dams were run, in water diversions and irrigation, in the discharge of municipal and industrial wastewater, and even in logging and ranching practices on the uplands. At last, in the 1990s, the public was interested in what scientists had to say about streams and watersheds.

The new scientific theories were all about connections and process. A healthy river is highly connected to its watershed in four dimensions: longitudinal (upstream-downstream); lateral (floodplain-uplands); vertical (surface water–groundwater); and through time, since the other connections are dynamic. You could say, then, that a river is connected to its watershed lengthwise, crosswise, and vertically, and that it changes over time, like a clay rope that is continually pulled and squeezed into new shapes.

A healthy river is linked in thousands of intricate ways with the surrounding landscape and with the water moving through that landscape. It periodically surges across its floodplain, carves new channels, abandons old ones, and carries away fallen trees. It tears away islands and terraces and piles up materials to build new ones. Groundwater from the surrounding uplands flows into the river, and the river water soaks into underground aquifers.

Rivers connect the entire landscape, from alpine meadows to the salty water of the estuaries. Pacific Northwest rivers link remote wildernesses and deserts to golfcourses and shopping malls.

The connections are all dynamic. A healthy river is tightly connected to its watershed, but it is not in a steady state. Its condition might more accurately be described as dynamic equilibrium. Disturbance is normal and, in fact, frequent. (However, our human activities in the watershed have changed the frequency and intensity of natural disturbances, and have also reduced the river's capacity to handle disturbance.) The river floods, creates new channels, is pummeled by landslides, and is occasionally disrupted by volcanic eruptions. As Heraclitus wrote, you cannot step into the same river twice. The river is constantly changing—that is the very nature of water.

A connected river is resilient. Through its rich network of ecological functions, it can process natural disturbances, like a stomach digesting food. It can absorb occasional landslides—which occur naturally in the steep mountains of the Pacific Northwest—because the large logjams in the river and the mature forests on its banks catch the moving mass of earth and rock before it scours much of the main channel. The logs and boulders from the slide renew the river's complex structure, the dirt is settled out in pools, and the organic matter is eaten by the thriving community of living organisms in the river.

It is not disturbance that destroys an ecosystem. It is when connections are broken that the health of the river suffers. When dams slice across the river, they sever vital connections. Returning salmon are blocked from their spawning streams. Logs and debris that would normally be washed downstream to contribute to the river's structure on lower stretches are trapped behind the dams and removed from the reservoirs by maintenance crews. Fish that live in the river year-round, such as bull and rainbow trout, are divided into separate, isolated populations. When reservoirs hold back water, they keep the river from flooding and disconnect it from its floodplain. When logjams are pulled out of rivers, or forests along river edges logged, or rivers channelized, links are cut between the rivers and their watersheds.

Every time a link is uncoupled, the river ecosystem is weakened a little more. Its ecological processes are interrupted or simplified. If enough connections are broken, the river dies. It may still look beautiful, but ecologically it functions like a culvert. It is simply a conduit for water passing through.

I'm close to home now. Just past milepost 50, I come into McKenzie Bridge. Jim's Oregon Whitewater has a placard out for guided rafting trips. A sign on the general store warns: "Last Gas for Fifty Miles." McKenzie Bridge has a few small, rustic lodges, places where people can stay after a day of rafting the river or hiking the McKenzie River Trail or doing catch-and-release fishing for the McKenzie redside rainbow trout.

Over the bridge, and still upriver from me, is the official Wild and Scenic McKenzie River. Just under thirteen miles of the upper river were designated as a federal wild and scenic river in 1988 as part of an omnibus bill that added segments of forty Oregon rivers to the federal wild and scenic rivers system. Newspapers announced that forty Oregon rivers had been "protected," but the Pacific Rivers Council, which had been instrumental in getting the bill passed, soon realized the protection was limited. Only short segments of rivers, usually upriver stretches on federally owned lands, were protected. The designation did not apply to headwater streams above, or to rivers downstream from the wild and scenic segments. In addition, the wild and scenic segments included only a narrow corridor averaging a quarter of a mile wide on each side of the riverbanks. Because upstream, downstream, and the uplands were not protected; because a river is connected to its entire watershed; and because water runs downhill, the "wild and scenic" designation did very little to protect the river and its ecosystem.

The Clean Water Act, another piece of federal environmental legislation, applied to the entire length of all rivers, but it merely required that the water be clean, not that it support any life. Pure, clean water running down a concrete trough would meet the Clean Water Act's requirements. The Pacific Rivers Council realized that a new approach was needed to protect rivers and the life in them—an approach based on watersheds.

The Forest Service was coming to the same conclusion. In the late 1980s and early 1990s, the federal agency was hit again and again with lawsuits, injunctions, court orders, and public protests. Its legal mandates required it to manage national forests for multiple use—that is, to produce timber while at the same time protecting wildlife and providing recreation. But managing the land for all purposes was becoming increasingly difficult. New species kept being listed as threatened and endangered—first the spotted owl, then the marbled murrelet. More species kept popping up as candidates for listing: red-legged frogs, white-footed voles, Townsend's big-eared bats. The habitat needs of all these species had to be met. Loggers objected that no one was looking out for the habitat needs of loggers. The Forest Service became doubly frustrated. Not only was it virtually impossible to plan a timber sale that satisfied every constraint, it was also impossible to carry out activities needed for good stewardship of the land, such as rehabilitation after forest fires. The agency realized that it needed a systemic approach to managing the national forests instead of the old piecemeal planning. Forest Service leaders starting talking about ecosystem management and watershed analysis. They, too, wanted to use an approach based on watersheds.

I'm not going on to the upper McKenzie today. I turn off the highway onto my road, then up my driveway. Douglas-firs and grand firs surround the log home where I live with my family. Every branch has a soft brush of new growth at the tip. Wild irises and false Solomon's seal are blooming around the fringes of the lawn where the forest starts.

I first fell in love with the McKenzie River in 1974. A college student from Buffalo, New York, I'd saved enough money to spend my summer vacation backpacking in the West. I'd been in the California mountains most of the summer, and the greenness of Oregon was like a refreshing

Natural logjams were removed to clear rivers for log drives, reducing a river's ability to digest floods (McKenzie River, 1909). (photo courtesy Lane County Historical Museum, L4B/L72-378A)

drink after the dry Sierra forests of pine and granite. I discovered the McKenzie River on my way to the Three Sisters Wilderness and fell in love with it. I moved to Oregon permanently in 1977, and I've lived in the McKenzie River Valley since 1980.

Though I loved to hike the McKenzie River Trail or raft the river, I knew very little about the river for many years. Not until 1987, when I was hiking with my friend Gene Skrine—he's still my friend, and since 1990 he's been my husband too—did I notice salmon swimming upstream to spawn, and then only because Gene pointed them out to me. The next year, the upper McKenzie was designated as a wild and scenic river, and the McKenzie Ranger District was given the responsibility of writing a management plan for the newly designated stretch. At the time, I worked for the Forest Service as a writer-editor and I was assigned to the river planning team as their writer, where I learned more about river issues.

A Forest Service official signed the decision notice that put our team's wild and scenic river plan into effect on January 9, 1992. Exactly one week later, a tanker truck carrying five thousand gallons of used motor oil slid into the ditch by Goodpasture Bridge, a covered bridge about twenty-five miles downstream from the wild and scenic upper McKenzie. Oil poured into the ditch and the culvert, and from the culvert into the river. Local volunteer firefighters and state highway crews were the first responders. They used loads of gravel and absorbent booms to soak up oil and keep it out of the river. Later, specialized crews took over. An oil slick started to drift downriver toward the trout hatchery, where trout ponds holding nearly a million fish were fed continuously by river water, and toward the salmon hatchery farther downstream and the water intake pipes for the city of Eugene's drinking water. The quick response and just plain luck saved the McKenzie from serious damage. Less than five hundred gallons of oil went into the river, and the floating booms kept it confined to a narrow strip along one bank. Still, the accident was a graphic demonstration to me that wild and scenic status for a corridor a few miles long did little to protect an entire river.

Rivers in wilderness areas are often our best examples of healthy rivers, like the North Fork of the John Day River. (Val Rapp)

I resigned from the Forest Service in 1993 to work as a freelance writer and writing consultant. I continued to learn about rivers and watersheds, and to explore the McKenzie River valley that is my home. The Pacific Rivers Council workshop I just attended is part of my self-education.

The questions that Charley Dewberry asked at the Pacific Rivers Council workshop seem to me to be the important questions to ask about the McKenzie River, and about all our Pacific Northwest rivers. What makes a river healthy? How badly are our rivers in the Pacific Northwest damaged? Can the wild salmon survive? Do we know enough to restore our rivers, and is there still time?

We have dammed, mined, logged, farmed, and built throughout our watersheds. We have disrupted and broken ecological connections. Have our rivers died—turned into beautiful culverts with sparkling water flowing through them—or are they still living, functioning ecosystems that could be restored to full health?

In this book, I will range widely through the Pacific Northwest, looking at stream ecology, river health, and the state of our rivers. I will return over and over to the McKenzie, because I live here and I love the river. Also, I want to explore my own connections with the river I know best. I believe that if we want to restore our rivers, we have to change our relationships with our rivers—our personal connections.

A close look at many Pacific Northwest rivers can lead a person to despair, or to pray for miracles. But if there is hope for rivers anywhere in the continental United States, it is here. Perhaps through the study of our rivers, I can connect to hope for rivers, for watersheds, for healthy landscapes where both the human and natural communities are flourishing.

Chapter 2

The Elegant Connection

When I first moved to the Pacific Northwest, I never asked if the rivers were healthy. They were beautiful. The upper McKenzie River plunged through forests of big Douglas-firs, western redcedars, and hemlocks. White water broke over boulders and foamed through rapids. Black basalt cliffs rose above the river mist. The water was so cold that just a splash made me suck in my breath sharply, and so clear that I could see the rocky bottom fifteen feet below. At the same time, the water was saturated with colors, azure blue in a pool, blue-green surging over a boulder, gray-green on an overcast day. When I walked the McKenzie River Trail, I walked among old-growth trees, wild rhododendrons, salal, moss-covered logs, and clumps of sword ferns. Sometimes I saw an osprey or a great blue heron, or a pair of mergansers.

As I explored my new home, I found that rivers in other parts of the Pacific Northwest were very different from the McKenzie. The John Day River in eastern Oregon wanders through canyons of red-brown rimrock with forests of scattered ponderosa pines, and farther downstream, open grasslands and sagebrush. Thick patches of grass edge the water with green, but the John Day is twined in my memory with the high-desert scents of pine resin and sagebrush.

The Hoh River on the Olympic Peninsula is whitish-blue with glacial flour carried from the Olympic Mountains. The river pushes the trees away from its banks, with several channels twisting, merging, and splitting again across a wide gravel floodplain. Where the Hoh finally allows the forest to approach, it is a rain forest with cedars and Douglas-firs ten feet or more in diameter, dwarfing the McKenzie's old growth.

The Illinois River in southwestern Oregon cuts a canyon through the granite and serpentinite of the Siskiyou Mountains before it flows into the Rogue River. Here, the familiar Douglas-fir is mixed with red fir, tanoak, knobcone pine, manzanita, poison oak, and the insect-eating California pitcher plant.

East of the Columbia Gorge, the Columbia River moves with solemn grandeur between basalt cliffs that parallel the river for miles. Beyond the cliffs is an austere landscape of tan bluffs covered with sparse grass that turns green only a few weeks of the year.

There are many more rivers besides these, and I never got tired of exploring them. Like people, the rivers were all unique. But was beautiful the same as healthy?

I wanted to know what healthy rivers looked like and how scientists defined healthy rivers. As I interviewed people for this book, I asked them for examples of healthy rivers—pristine rivers with intact ecosystems. I questioned scientists who had spent years studying rivers in the Pacific Northwest and fish biologists working for state and federal agencies, the men and women who knew an area's rivers the best.

A field biologist on the Olympic Peninsula was silent for a few seconds before answering me. "I've been here twenty-two years," he said, "and there was a lot of timber harvest even before my existence, so no area is exactly pristine, exactly what it should be. But we do still have rivers that have significantly high-quality natural environment." He mentioned the Soleduck, the Hoh, and upper Elwha Rivers, all on the Olympic Peninsula. "I love the upper Elwha," he said. "There's a beautiful valley higher up that I think is prime spring chinook habitat." But, he pointed out, the upper Elwha River is blocked by two dams built in the early 1900s without fish passage. Salmon haven't been able to reach the prime habitat of the upper Elwha for over eighty years. The upper river is pristine, but missing a key part of its ecosystem.

A researcher studying the differences between streams in logged and unlogged watersheds told me that he had trouble finding the latter. The Olympic Peninsula, he said, had the best possibilities for healthy rivers. He mentioned the Hoh River, but then added that the lower Hoh ran through commercial timberland that had all been logged. I wouldn't have to be a scientist to see that the heavy logging changed the river ecosystem, he said: the difference was dramatic at the Olympic National Park boundary.

All the answers I got followed the same pattern: first, silence for a few seconds, then names of rivers—the Hoh, Elwha, and Quinalt Rivers on the Olympic Peninsula; the Chiwawa River in eastern Washington; the Rogue River in southern Oregon; Cummins Creek in the Oregon Coast

Range; the McKenzie River in the Oregon Cascades; the North Fork of the John Day River in eastern Oregon; the Salmon River in Idaho. But the names always came with qualifiers: the rivers were "relatively healthy," people told me; or "not pristine but better than some others"; or they had good habitat higher up, but dams on their lower reaches.

When I looked closely, I couldn't find any completely pristine rivers with unaltered ecosystems in the Pacific Northwest. The upper parts of some watersheds were protected in wilderness areas, but the lower watersheds had been changed in many ways—by logging, roads, towns, and agriculture. Many rivers had dams on their lower reaches, interfering with or completely blocking salmon runs that used to return to the upper reaches. Wilderness streams in the high Cascades were still recovering

A complex channel, driftwood logs, gravel bars, and a streamside forest create habitat diversity and a biological hotspot along the McKenzie River. (Val Rapp)

from heavy sheep grazing at the turn of the century.

Many wilderness streams had exotic, introduced fish species like brook trout or were regularly planted with hatchery fish. Often the remaining wild fish now carried diseases introduced by hatchery fish or exotics. Overfishing outside the watershed had decimated the salmon runs of many rivers, changing them ecologically in ways that couldn't be seen by looking at the rivers. Species whose life cycle depended on the salmon, like the western pearlshell clam, were often missing. Animals that once played key ecological roles were gone or scarce—such as beavers, which were still recovering from overtrapping in the late 1800s. All the rivers had been touched by Western civilization. Something was missing, or something was added, or something was changed.

But some streams and rivers were almost pristine—we hadn't changed them very much. The upper Hoh was protected by Olympic National Park. Its lower reaches, while not pristine, were undammed and flowed freely to the ocean. The Hoh still had six different wild salmon and steelhead runs, with minimal hatchery influence. Cummins Creek flowed out of a small watershed on the Oregon coast. Only one small piece of its watershed had been logged in the past, and most of the drainage was now designated as wilderness. There were others, the rivers that people had named when I asked. The "almost pristine" rivers would have to be my models for healthy rivers.

THE MCKENZIE WATERSHED

Separation Creek begins as a dribble of meltwater from the glaciers and snowfields of the Middle and South Sisters. From these peaks in the McKenzie watershed, it trickles across a plain of volcanic rock and alpine flowers, then drops down through the forest, mountain hemlock at first, then Pacific silver fir, and eventually Douglas-fir at lower elevations. Separation Creek Falls is a beautiful cascade of fifty feet or so. Below the falls, the creek stair-steps down a steep canyon, plunging over fallen trees and boulders into small pools in a wild, exuberant descent thousands of feet long. The narrow, V-shaped canyon holds the stream in almost a straight line. Occasionally the mountain slope is gentle for a few hundred feet, and the stream spreads out to create a small swamp overgrown with brush.

What I notice the most about walking along an almost pristine stream is that the going gets difficult once I'm off the trail. I have to climb over logs, struggle through brush, and detour around side channels. I've walked different parts of Separation Creek at different times. Right now, I'm walking along the stream's lower reaches in May, through an old-growth Douglas-fir forest. Last winter's high winds blew a few trees down across the stream. Other trees lost their hold on the rain-saturated slopes during heavy rainstorms and tore out by the roots. Trees, rocks, and dirt slid down into the stream. Splintered pieces of new wood are piled up against older logjams. The oldest logs are spongy with rot. Every piece of small wood that I pick up from the stream has tiny creatures on it, mostly aquatic insect larvae that squirm away from me in the film of water clinging to the wood. A hatch of some kind of midge or fly hovers over rotten logs on a side channel. The stream and its banks are rich with texture and complexity. I touch the rough bark of newly fallen trees, the light yellow wood of freshly broken chunks. I walk among Douglas-firs six feet in diameter and saplings I could break with my hands, vine maples and alders leafing out, trilliums and fairybells blooming, devil's club, and red currant. The water moves through an endless complexity of pools, riffles, cascades, and eddies.

Separation Creek pours into Horse Creek, doubling the latter's size. The wider stream is only partially shaded by the trees on its banks, and the water sparkles in the sunlight. No longer constrained by the narrow canyon and no longer plunging headfirst down a steep mountain, the creek cuts a more complex channel, with small meanders, gravel bars, and a few small islands. Horse Creek cut a new channel through one island in last winter's flood, dug its main channel deeper in places, and left new deposits of gravel piled around alder trunks on some bars.

Horse Creek flows into the McKenzie River, and several miles below their confluence, the South Fork of the McKenzie flows into the mainstem. The river is not completely pristine here. Cougar Dam straddles the South Fork, regulating its water flow, and the McKenzie Highway flanks one side of the river. Houses, lawns, and managed forests are scattered across the valley, but much of the South Fork delta area, as this region is called, is fairly intact. The McKenzie has developed a complex maze of channels in its wider valley. Side channels wind through the forest. Along the main channel, crescents of alders flank the curves. The dark green and much taller Douglas-firs stand behind the alders. Gravel bars sprawl along the inside edges of curves while on the opposite, outside edges, the current sweeps past forested banks. A large logjam has formed off the end of one bar, anchored by several large trees. Driftwood logs are scattered across the bars and islands, and along the banks in some places.

Scattered depressions in the long gravel bars hold shallow pools. The river actually flows under and through the gravel, so the pools have cold, fresh water. Each one is full of life. Caddisfly larvae walk along the bottom, their six tiny legs dragging cases built from fir needles, tiny bits of wood, and grains of sand. As soon as I stick my hand in the water, they pull into their shelters, which now look like lifeless bits of debris. A snail tucks into its spiral-shaped dark brown shell, and a number of small, light brown crustaceans scoot backward and under rocks so fast I cannot get a good look at them.

Here at the South Fork delta, the McKenzie is already a partially engineered river. It becomes even more controlled downstream. To see an (almost) pristine large river in a lowland valley, I'll have to look somewhere else. But before I do, I want to understand what the streams of the McKenzie watershed can teach me about healthy rivers.

Researchers have studied the McKenzie watershed closely. Forest Service scientists began research projects in the H.J. Andrews Experimental Forest when it was established in 1948. At first they examined mainly logging and road system designs. By the 1960s, their focus had shifted to watersheds and the effects of logging on water quality and yield. In the 1970s, they focused more on forest and stream ecology, beginning the long-term work needed to understand how these ecosystems actually worked.

Over the years the Forest Service scientists, with offices in Corvallis, Oregon, developed close working relationships with scientists from Oregon State University, also in Corvallis. The H.J. Andrews also became part of a national long-term ecological research program funded by the National Science Foundation. The Forest Service and university researchers produced a long list of scientific journal articles, dissertations, and presentations at scientific conferences. Mack Creek and Lookout Creek in the H.J. Andrews became probably the most thoroughly studied streams in the Pacific Northwest. Many projects used other streams in the McKenzie watershed as additional study sites, including the McKenzie itself, and the field work accomplished in the watershed helped produce some of the key concepts of modern stream ecology.

The McKenzie watershed research built on principles established by hydrologists in the 1950s and 1960s. The hydrologists had begun with the obvious—water flows downhill and rivers meander—and asked what the scientific significance was.

Water flows downhill in the easiest way it can find. Gravity pulls the water down, and friction resists the flow. While rivers are shaped partly by the landscape, they also shape themselves in response to gravity and friction.

Decaying alder leaves and their coating of fungi and bacteria are like crackers and peanut butter to the food web in streams. (Val Rapp)

On steep mountain slopes, the easiest path for water is straight downhill. But this path generates tremendous erosive force—think of a jet of water spewing out of a downspout and cutting into the ground. The stair-step structure that I saw in upper Separation Creek dissipates much of the erosive force. By dropping over many small steps into many small pools, the water is able to come straight down the mountain without slicing into it deeply. Erosion would add dirt to the water, which would create more work for the stream in two ways: the current would have to carry the bedload, and the sediment would create additional friction. Obedient to the laws of physics, the stream conserves energy and takes a stair-step form that minimizes erosion.

Once a river is out of the mountains, the easiest way for its waters to go downhill is to meander. The familiar curve of a river meander is a shape that we recognize immediately. Any seven-year-old can draw it. Scientists have described it in ratios that hold true for watercourses of all sizes, from small creeks to large rivers. The meander curve minimizes erosion in the flatter landscape of a valley, and again allows the river to take a course that expends the least energy. The exact form of any particular river is always a compromise between its tendency to meander and the surrounding geography.

Water flows the fastest on the outside of the curve, and here its greater force scoops out pools and erodes the bank. Water travels slower on the inside of a curve, where it drops any gravel and sand it's carrying, forming a gravel bar like the ones I saw in the delta area of the McKenzie River. The bar deflects the water back toward the opposite bank, where the water initiates another bend. Thus a river meanders across its valley in sinuous curves. Below the surface, the riverbed undulates up and down, with pools and riffles alternating from side to side along the meanders.

The McKenzie watershed researchers took the hydrologists' findings and brought them to life. They found that a river's biological patterns are closely connected to its physical patterns in an intricate system that is both elegant and beautiful.

Stan Gregory, a professor of fisheries and wildlife at Oregon State University, has been doing research in the McKenzie watershed since 1971. He leads the "Stream Team"—if the group can be said to have a leader—a loosely connected group of professors at Oregon State who have researched stream ecology over the last twenty years. I'm riding with Stan and several fish biologists on our way to see a fish population study in Quartz Creek in the McKenzie watershed. The streams of this watershed are familiar to me, but I want to learn what the biologists see. I want to see more than just how beautiful these streams are.

"I've learned things by staying in the McKenzie drainage since 1971," Stan tells me. "I feel you get to know the system this way. One criticism I get of the H.J. research is that it's an ecology of the H.J. Andrews, not the Pacific Northwest. But I think it's a good foundation. I go to other systems to compare."

The Stream Team discovered that rivers change biologically from their headwaters to the ocean, just as they change physically. Food—energy—is the foundation of the ecosystem. In headwater streams such as Separation Creek, the forest along the stream is the main energy source. The Douglas-firs, hemlocks, and cedars shade the narrow stream. Without sunlight, few algae grow and aren't much of a basis for a food chain. But the forest showers the stream with a steady source of nutrients. The fallen trees and the litter of needles, leaves, and sticks provide a rich food base, but one that most animals cannot digest.

Just as the Serengeti Plain is crowded with herds of grazing zebras, the small streams are full of browsing creatures. Stonefly larvae shred leaves into pieces, beetle larvae gouge tunnels into logs, and snails move along the film of algae and fungi on the bark, rasping off the soft outer layers of wood. Grazers and shredders break down the leaves and wood into smaller pieces. Leaves may be processed through the stream system in less than a year, whereas a large log may take centuries. These aquatic insect larvae—the tiny beings that squirmed and crawled over every stick and branch in Separation Creek—digest very little of the fiber, passing along most of it in the form of droppings into the water. They're also an important food source themselves for the salamanders, fish, and predatory insects that are the hunters of this watery Serengeti.

The Stream Team biologists asked, What else goes downstream besides water? They found that an organic soup of shredded bits of wood and leaves, insect droppings, and other debris flows down from small streams into larger ones.

Here on Quartz Creek, our group starts wading upstream. Stan cautions me to avoid stepping on areas of pebbles and sand in shallow water, explaining that the cutthroat trout pick these spots to make their redds, or nests. The cutthroat laid their eggs several months ago, and now in June the young fry are just emerging out of the spawning gravels into the stream itself. Although the pebbles keep the tiny fish safe from predators, the fry could be crushed by our feet. I'm not equipped with felt-soled waders like most of the group and am struggling to stay upright, wet to my hips in the cold water. Sighing, I avoid the gravels that gave me solid footing and instead pick my way through the uneven cobble of the main channel and scramble across slick boulders.

Quartz Creek is smaller than Horse Creek, but it falls into the same general category of midsized streams. It's wide enough that the forest doesn't shade it completely. More sunlight reaches the water, and more algae grow than in the narrow headwater streams. Food drifts down from the smaller streams in a constant flow of shredded wood and leaves and animal droppings. Living things travel downstream too, from aquatic insect larvae knocked loose into the current to migrating young fish. During freshets, the rising water carries a wealth of materials—gravel, sand, dirt, leaves, sticks, and driftwood logs. The richness and variety of nutrients create a more complex food web in the midsized streams than existed in Separation Creek. Midsized streams also have a greater diversity of habitats: driftwood logs piled up in logjams, boulders, pools of different sizes, riffles, quiet eddies, side channels, and a streambed with areas of sand, gravel, cobble, and bedrock. The roughness of the stream, the complexity that makes it so difficult for me to walk up Quartz Creek, creates a patchy mosaic of habitats. A rich biological community lives, eats, and dies in this complex ecosystem.

We poke around in the stream while we're walking up Quartz Creek, to see what's swimming around on this overcast June day. I pick up a stone from a shallow riffle and turn it over. "Mayfly," says Dave, a biologist, pointing to the brown creature clinging to the rock's underside. The nymph has three graceful tail filaments and gills along its abdomen. I place the stone back into the water gently. The nymph may be able to hold on to it or may be dislodged into the current to float downstream until it can grab a new rock—unless it's first eaten by a hungry trout.

We see juga snails—small black mollusks grazing on the film of algae that covers the rocks—and caddisfly larvae. Several of us crouch around a small pool below a boulder on the stream's edge. "There's a cutthroat fry," Stan says. I can't see it. "There's another one," he notes. By the time he's spotted three, I finally see one, and once I'm able to pick out one, I can see the others. The little fish are almost transparent, like tiny slivers of light in the water. They move their tails slightly from side to side, holding themselves in the shallow water near the stream margin, where larger, predatory fish can't get at them. Stan counts five cutthroat fry just in this one small pool. "The redd may be close to this pool," he says. "They may have just emerged and haven't dispersed any farther yet."

Then Stan detects a predator that could hunt the cutthroat fry in these shallows. He points to a crevice under a rock on the pool's edge: "Pacific giant salamander." I have to move a little before I can see it lurking. The immature amphibian is greenish, with a fringe of gills around its neck. From its hiding place it hunts young fish, insects, and other small aquatic animals. As an adult, its gills will disappear, its skin will develop a mottled pattern, and it will move to the land, living under logs or rocks in the forest.

The Pacific giant salamander splits its life between the stream and the land. Like the entire aquatic community, it depends on both a healthy stream and a healthy forest. One of Stan Gregory's and the Stream Team's most important contributions to stream ecology has been an understanding of the significance of riparian zones. It's only in the last twenty years that biologists have begun to understand how much fish need trees.

The riparian zone is the ribbon of land next to the stream where land and stream interact. This zone is much more than the banks that define the stream's active channel or the area where plants tolerant of a high water table, such as willows and alders, grow. It is a three-dimensional area of complex linkages between land and stream. Where a stream is constrained by a narrow canyon, the riparian area is squeezed down to a narrow band. In an unconstrained reach, the zone encompasses the wider floodplain.

The riparian zone is a complex system made up of patches of forest, side channels, gravel bars, and islands. The streamside forest controls the amount of shade or sunlight reaching the water, stabilizes the banks during floods, filters the groundwater seeping into the stream, provides leaves and wood to the aquatic food web, and is the source of large logs for the stream. The stream provides a high water table and moist soils for the riparian area. The stream uses and shapes the riparian zone most during seasonal flooding, when it pours down old side channels, cuts new ones, creates openings by taking out groups of trees, renews links to sloughs and wetlands, and recruits trees and organic debris into the channel.

Water flows downhill. But movement occurs both upstream and downstream in the riparian zone. Animals as diverse as bats, beavers, and elk use the riparian ribbon as a migration corridor. When the insect larvae living in the stream mature, the adult stoneflies, caddisflies, mayflies, and dozens of other insects leave its eddies for the breezes and winds of the air. Many species use the riparian corridors to fly upstream to lay their eggs, a migration that compensates for the inevitable downstream drift of the insect larvae.

The continuous ribbon of the riparian corridor is also an aggregate of patches: forest of different ages and species—alder and willow, Douglas-fir, and cedar—and open gravel bars, wetlands, sloughs, and islands. This mosaic is the result of past floods, the height of the water table, and the ground type, which might be soil, sand, or cobble. The Stream Team found that streams with complex riparian zones—with a lot of patchiness—were hotspots of biological productivity. Complex riparian zones had twice the number of plant species as upland areas, and streams that flowed through these diversified areas had twice as many trout as streams with simpler riparian edges.

The Stream Team's work in the McKenzie watershed built an important foundation, and their research was confirmed and expanded on by other scientists in other watersheds. The old idea that streams were simply channels that carried rain and snow runoff to the ocean was discarded. The new science of river ecology found that streams have complicated patterns of downstream and upstream flow. The downstream flow of water is continuous, but in a healthy stream it is frequently interrupted by logs, boulders, and meanders. The roughness that makes it so difficult for me to walk up these streams creates diversity. The logjams catch food such as alder leaves and hold the leaves long enough for stonefly nymphs to shred them and for fish to eat the nymphs. The insect and fish droppings and bits of shredded leaves continue downstream, to be caught again in another spot and recycled yet another time. It's as if a stream had a thousand stomachs and digested a little bit of its food in each one. Meanwhile, adult salmon and trout migrate upstream to spawn, and other animals migrate up and down through the riparian corridor. Healthy streams have two apparently contradictory tendencies: the continuity of

At the mouth of the Hoh River, driftwood logs cover the beach. Historically, most Pacific Northwest rivers had this much wood at their mouths. (Val Rapp)

the water flowing downstream, and the structural roughness that interrupts the flow and turns the stream into a patchwork of diverse habitats.

The patterns are repeated from watershed to watershed across the Pacific Northwest, from stair-stepping streams in the mountains to meandering rivers in the valleys. The headwater streams of the Oregon Cascades are similar in ecological patterns to the headwater streams of the Idaho Bitterroots, the North Cascades, the Olympics, and the Coast Ranges. The rivers—the John Day, Illinois, Deschutes, Hoh, Wenatchee, and dozens of others—share structural and ecological similarities. But the rivers and their ecosystems are also different from one another, as individual as the mountain ranges, forests, and deserts that birthed them. Like human beings, each river system is a unique expression of a general template.

Has stream ecology found the answers, then, about how stream ecosystems work? When Stan was driving our group up to Quartz Creek, he told me he thinks stream ecology is just coming out of its infancy:

In the 1950s and 1960s, stream ecology was a young science. It's now a more sophisticated discipline and has more links to other ecological disciplines. But we're still a long ways from a unified theory in ecological disciplines.

I really hope that in twenty years people will say, "Those idiots in the nineties, why didn't they know this?" This being whatever they've learned by then. I hope they've learned new stuff in twenty years.

THE HOH RIVER

The headwater streams of the Hoh River curl around the east, north, and west sides of Mount Olympus, the highest peak of the Olympics, like vine tendrils around a tree trunk. Mount Olympus gets an average of 200 inches of snow and rain every year, and the Hoh River valley averages 145 inches of rain each year, twice as much as the McKenzie Valley's average 70 to 75 inches. The rain forest of the Hoh River valley dwarfs the old-growth forest of the upper McKenzie watershed. Sitka spruce, western redcedars, and Douglas-firs are commonly ten or more feet in diameter. Ferns and mosses hang from the trees.

I'm here to see an almost pristine large river in a lowland valley, something I can't see in the developed lower McKenzie and Willamette Valleys. I'm alone; I have no guide to interpret what I'm seeing in terms of what I've read in scientific journals. The Hoh's headwaters and much of its mainstem are protected in Olympic National Park. The lower river runs through privately owned timberland that has been heavily logged and is now covered by second- and third-growth forest. The land north of the river mouth is included in the narrow strip of Olympic National Park that runs along the Pacific coast, and the land south of the river mouth is in the Hoh Indian Reservation.

I spend the morning driving a dirt road to the mouth of the Hoh River where it flows into the Pacific Ocean, and walking on the shore. I see four immature bald eagles on the sand, almost full-grown, but their feathers still the mottled coloring of juveniles. A few minutes later I see two adult bald eagles. The beach is a couple of hundred feet wide at the river mouth and is covered with a deep layer of logs, rootwads, and branches. A lot of the driftwood logs are the remains of old-growth trees, three to eight feet in diameter, while others are skinny alder trunks. Broken chunks of all sizes are littered several feet deep. I could walk across the entire beach on the wood without ever touching the ground.

In the afternoon, some miles upriver, I hike a trail that winds up the Hoh Valley, leaving the path frequently to explore the river's edge. The Hoh dominates its wide floodplain, and several channels braid in and out of each other, winding among large, long gravel bars. Many bars are bare or have only a few young willows on them. Alder stands of various ages grow on others and border the outermost channel at the floodplain's edge. Driftwood logs are scattered over the floodplain's expanse of cobble, gravel, and sand. The rain forest begins beyond it. The river is a milky blue, white with rock flour ground from the glaciers of Mount Olympus and blue from clarity.

As large rivers typically do, the Hoh has created a broad floodplain. The river has little direct interaction with the forest, which is only a fringe along the Hoh's wide channels. The river actively shapes its branches and reworks its floodplain with periodic floods. It erodes, but it also builds in other spots, leaving deposits of gravel and sand as often as it cuts new courses. Although leaves, sticks, and logs still fall into the current, it also receives much organic matter carried downstream. The Hoh River is too deep and fast for me to wade in very far and turn over stones, but I would probably find different species of fish and a different mix of aquatic insect larvae, with more species that collect or filter the shredded bits of organic debris drifting in the current. The enormous amount of driftwood that I saw at the river mouth is the legacy of an almost pristine river still forested along most of its length.

The braided channels that I see are only the surface of the river. In just the last few years, scientists have found that in gravel-bed rivers like the

An unseen river of subsurface water flows beneath the wide floodplain of the Hoh and other large rivers, forming an "interstitial highway" through the gravels. (Val Rapp)

Hoh, the subsurface water flow can extend beneath much of the floodplain and may carry as much or more water than the surface river. Measurements on the Flathead River in Montana found that the water flow below the active channels averaged three kilometers wide and ten meters deep—an unseen river whose existence was not even suspected twenty years ago. The subsurface water upwells into the river and downwells back into the gravels at many places, entering and leaving the river many times. A side channel that appears to have only a trickle of water may carry a large subterranean flow.

This unseen river forms an "interstitial highway" that runs through the loose gravels of the floodplain. Preliminary research has discovered a food web of over eighty species living in this underground watercourse. The nymphs of several stonefly species have been found in water samples taken from monitoring wells as far as three kilometers from the actual river channel.

I can't see the hidden river flowing beneath the gravel bar where I'm standing, but I imagine the Hoh as being like the soaking garden hose I have at home. The hose carries water, and it also oozes water continuously through the hose jacket. The river is even more permeable than the hose, and it both oozes and absorbs water. The river is like a soaker hose carrying flowing water, but without any hose jacket at all, completely permeable to the surrounding landscape.

THE STREAM NETWORK

We tend to think of ecosystems as collections of living organisms in particular places. We forget that an ecosystem actually includes the nonliving environment as well as the biological community. It's easy to talk about a river as if it is alive—a healthy organism, digesting its food in a thousand stomachs—but the river isn't alive. It's a physical system of water, rock, and dirt, and the water is always obedient to its physical imperative: seek the easiest way downhill. But it is nevertheless impossible to separate the physical river from its biological community.

An ecologist from a federal agency spoke to me about "the elegance of the connections between the physical and biological systems." The driftwood logs that were once trees, that are now crawling with algae and snails and tunneling beetle larvae, form logjams that help to shape the river's intricate physical structure. The biological community is superbly adapted to thrive in a varied system of pools, meanders, and riffles. So it makes sense to talk about river health because the river and its biota are inseparable—the sparkling blue-green water and the cutthroat trout holding in the pool.

Chapter 3

Disturbance and Resilience

ater offers no resistance to anything in its path. The *Tao Te Ching* says, "There is nothing softer and weaker than water, and yet there is nothing better for attacking hard and strong things." Made of water and seeking only to go downhill, rivers are soft and weak.

Yet rivers are the most enduring feature of our landscape. The Columbia is older than the Cascades. It flowed to the ocean before the mountains ever existed. The broad arch of the range rose slowly over millions of years, spiked by volcanoes like Mount Rainier, Mount Adams, and Mount Hood. But the Columbia sliced a gorge through the rock barrier as fast as peaks rose in its path and continued to flow to the ocean, the only river that actually cuts through the Cascades.

At least twice after the major peaks were built, lava flows from Cascades volcanoes dammed the Columbia Gorge. Each time, behind the lava dam, the river formed a lake of unknown size but eventually eroded through the lava and cut a course through the gorge again.

Eighteen thousand years ago, during the Pleistocene epoch, or Ice Age, the northern third of Washington was almost all under ice. The huge Cordilleran ice sheet covered the northern end of the Olympic Peninsula, lay like a broad tongue across Puget Sound and the lowlands west of the Cascades, and reached across the Okanogan area, parts of northeastern Washington, northern Idaho, and northern Montana. The Cascades peaks stood out like islands in a sea of white. South of the main ice sheet, glaciers spread down the flanks of mountains like Mount Hood and the Three Sisters and filled the upper ends of the valleys radiating from the summits.

The headwaters of many Pacific Northwest rivers were covered by glaciers, and in northern Washington, entire watersheds were under ice. Rivers emerged from under the edges of the ice sheet and flowed across gravel plains. A glacier blocked the Columbia in northern Washington, causing the river to yield and change its course. For centuries, it flowed down a gorge now known as the Grand Coulee and over a waterfall almost four hundred feet high and more than three miles across. By the end of the Ice Age, though, the glacier had melted back far enough for the Columbia to return to its original course, leaving the Grand Coulee a dry riverbed.

By thirteen thousand years before the present, the Cordilleran ice sheet was in retreat. In what is now the Idaho Panhandle, one lobe of the sheet dammed the Clark Fork River. Water filled the valleys of present-day western Montana, forming Glacial Lake Missoula. Eventually, the lake became deep enough to float the ice dam. When the dam lifted, the water emptied in a huge torrent over eastern Washington and the Columbia River valley. Geologists estimate that the glacial lake held about as much water as modern Lake Ontario and that the flood formed a wall of water two thousand feet high, draining the basin completely in less than two weeks.

After the lake drained, the ice dropped back into its former position, where it again formed a barrier, and the impounded waters began to build behind it once more. Geologists calculate that Glacial Lake Missoula filled and emptied more than forty times over a timespan of roughly fifteen hundred years as the ice dam repeatedly floated and dropped. Forty enormous floods cut stream channels hundreds of feet deep across eastern Washington, leaving plateaus of soft, yellow soil like islands among canyons scraped to black basalt bedrock. The floods tore away the lower ends of valleys in the Columbia Gorge and left dozens of streams to end abruptly in waterfalls, the best known of which is Multnomah Falls. Bottlenecks in the river canyons backed up the water until it could drain through. The Snake River swelled to six hundred feet deep, the Pasco Basin at Wallula Gap filled to one thousand feet, and the northern half of the Willamette Valley turned into a temporary lake four hundred feet deep.

On the Washington side of the Columbia Gorge, layers of basaltic rock from old lava flows lie on a middle band of soil, which in turn lies on older volcanic rock. All the layers of rock slope down toward the Columbia, and the band of soil acts like a lubricant. The upper layers tend to slide over the older strata and down into the river, like stacked, greased tiles slipping off a tipped table. Roughly six to seven hundred years ago, an enormous landslide crashed down into the Columbia Gorge between the present-day towns of North Bonneville and Stevenson. Millions of tons of rock dammed the river. A temporary lake formed behind the rock dam, but eventually the Columbia cut its way through the slide. Many trees that drowned in the lake were standing snags when Lewis and Clark came down the river in 1805. The old slide still crowds the Columbia against the Oregon shore and forms the narrows where Bonneville Dam was built. The reservoir behind the dam covers another remnant of the slide, the boulders that once formed the Cascades of the Columbia.

The Columbia was not the only river to survive geologic upheavals. The rugged landscape of the Pacific Northwest took its shape from large-scale, catastrophic disturbances. Volcanic eruption created the Cascades' stunning, snow-capped peaks—Mount Lassen, Mount Shasta, the Three Sisters, Mount Hood, Mount Saint Helens, Mount Rainier, Glacier Peak, and Mount Baker. The eruptions also filled river valleys with lava and mudflows, disrupted river drainages, and loaded the rivers with ashes and mud.

Mount Rainier, the 14,410-foot volcano that dominates Seattle's southern horizon, has a history of eruptions and mudflows in just the last few thousand years. About five thousand years ago, part of Rainier collapsed and slid down the White River valley to the northwest. The mudflow spread across more than a hundred square miles of the Puget Sound lowland in what is now the Enumclaw area. Roughly twenty-five hundred years ago, a series of eruptions built the small summit cone that exists today. Although these outbursts were small, the lava flows melted large parts of Rainier's glaciers, enormous mudflows surged down some of the valleys radiating from the mountain, and an avalanche of hot rock poured down Puyallup Valley.

The Northwest landscape is not a finished work. The forces that created it are still tearing down and rebuilding the mountains and valleys. Over the last four thousand years, Cascades volcanoes have erupted roughly twice each century. Floods, landslides, mudflows, and forest fires chisel and reconstruct the land. Rivers full of life have always been part of this dynamic landscape. Rivers yield to stone and lava, but they endure because they are resilient.

REFUGIA

A salmon egg is a fragile thing—a small, pinkish-red sphere with two tiny black eye dots. At some stages of its development, I could easily crush it between my thumb and forefinger if I lifted it from its gravel nest in the streambed. A cutthroat fry, a stonefly nymph, a Pacific giant salamander—these bits of flesh are fragile and easily destroyed. They could be crushed by rocks rolling along the bottom in a flood or squashed under the heel of a hiker wading across the stream on a summer day.

The five Pacific salmon species we have today, however, have existed for somewhere between five hundred thousand and 2 million years. During those 2 million years, the Pacific Northwest has gone through ten to twenty ice ages and unknown numbers of volcanic eruptions, postglaciation floods, landslides, and other disturbances. Like rivers, living things are soft and unresisting in comparison to hard, strong things like mountains, glaciers, and lava flows. But chinook and salamanders and stoneflies have not only survived in this dynamic landscape with all its upheavals. They have thrived—creating the robust ecosystems I saw in the almost pristine rivers. To understand healthy rivers, I need to understand how life responds to catastrophe.

Mount Saint Helens used to have one of the most symmetrical cones in the Cascades, but in 1980 it turned from one of the most shapely into one of the most interesting peaks. Swarms of small earthquakes began around the mountain on March 20, and a week later the volcano started to vent steam and small amounts of ash. As the minor eruptions continued, its north shoulder began to swell like a growing tumor.

On the morning of May 18, 1980, the snow melted rapidly from the enlarged mountainside, and the ground over the bulge began to quiver. Mount Saint Helens erupted with a force twenty-one thousand times that of the atomic bomb dropped on Hiroshima, and the entire upper thirteen hundred feet of the mountain disappeared, exploded into fragments. The north side collapsed and slid down into the North Fork of the Toutle River, filling Spirit Lake with mud and debris. The mudflow continued down the Toutle to the Cowlitz, and down the Cowlitz to the Columbia. The next day an oceangoing ship in the Columbia ran aground. Overnight, mud and debris had reduced the depth of the shipping channel from forty feet to about fifteen feet, over forty miles from the actual eruption. The mudflow had filled an entire river with mud, rock, and ash.

Mount Saint Helens was a major volcanic event in a scientific era. The early, small eruptions had attracted scientists who were in place around the mountain to observe and record what happened after the blast. While some men and women studied the mountain itself, others were interested in how living organisms responded to the destruction. The spring run of salmon in the Cowlitz River was expected to come in soon after the

May 18 eruption, and some biologists thought that the fish would come up the mud-filled river and die before spawning. But, in fact, the Cowlitz salmon—a hatchery run identifiable from its tags—showed up in the Kalama River, the next river upstream on the Columbia. The salmon did what other generations of salmon must have done thousands of times before. They avoided a river temporarily devastated and sought out the next river in the watershed with usable habitat.

The blast zone around Mount Saint Helens after May 18 was a barren landscape. The force of the eruption had knocked down the trees on thousands of acres, glowing ash flows had scorched the ground with a killing heat, and a thick layer of ash covered everything. In the Toutle and Cowlitz Rivers, the mudflow must have buried fish, amphibians, and insect larvae alive. The ones not buried suffocated as their gills clogged with silt and jagged-edged ash that cut like glass.

But not everything died. Some headwater streams were covered with ice at the time of the eruption, protecting trout and other aquatic animals from the scorching heat. In headwater streams, tributaries, and side-channel springs, the fish, amphibians, and insect larvae were sheltered from the scour and turbidity of the mudflow. Later, as the streams cleared up, these survivors began to recolonize the devastated rivers.

Ice offered safety during the Mount Saint Helens eruption, but during the Ice Age, ice was the problem. The ice sheet that covered northern Washington forced salmon out of thousands of miles of rivers. Salmon runs displaced from rivers buried in ice found places of refuge, or refugia, in the lower Columbia and its ice-free tributaries, in the Chehalis Basin in western Washington, and in river basins south of the Columbia. However, the ice sheet entombed the northern rivers for thousands of years, far too long for any salmon to have the memory or instinct to return to those rivers.

The ice did not go gently when it melted. Once it had retreated from a watershed, the rivers left behind were rocky channels, often filled with gravel and silt. Huge floods from glacial lakes scraped river channels bare, sometimes for hundreds of miles and sometimes repeatedly over hundreds of years. The surging waters must have wiped out virtually all river life time and again just as it was building.

"The streams were sterile," paleoscience consultant Jim Chatters explained to me. "Salmon take a long time to recolonize sterile streams." Jim has done extensive paleontological research in the Columbia River basin, reconstructing the ecological history of the rivers and of the salmon runs. Over the past ten thousand years, every component of the river ecosystems had to rebuild—complex, meandering channels and pools, riffles, and stable spawning gravels. Enough soil had to build up on the riverbanks for trees to grow, stabilize banks, drop leaves and needles into the water, and eventually fall into the currents and drift into logjams. A food web had to build.

The refugia were a long way from the rivers that were now free of ice, and it may have taken hundreds of years for some species to reach the developing habitats. Adult stoneflies are clumsy flyers and generally don't travel very far before they mate and die. The same is true for many other insects whose young live in streams. Aquatic snails spend their entire lives in the water and only crawl short distances in their lifetimes.

Distance wasn't a problem for salmon, strong swimmers that normally travel hundreds of miles home to spawn. But the salmon were in a "Catch-22" situation. Salmon runs wouldn't rebuild until the rivers had a food base that would support salmon fry, but the decaying bodies of adult salmon, which die after they spawn, are a major source of the nutrients that support that food base. So the salmon runs couldn't rebuild until the stoneflies and other invertebrates were there, and these organisms couldn't build large populations until salmon runs returned. Thus the salmon reclaimed the new habitats gradually, together with a slowly migrating biological community. An added difficulty was that once the rivers had recovered enough to support salmon, the salmon needed to stray from their birth streams into the newly available waterways. Finally, a natural global warming occurred from nine thousand to six thousand years ago: the winter snowpack was smaller, stream flows dropped, and water temperatures were warmer in the summer, all factors that held down the abundance of salmon populations in the Columbia River basin. But then the climate cooled. Rivers gushed with cold water and forests reclaimed the lower elevations that had been too dry for trees to survive during the period of warmer climate.

"The salmon population exploded about four thousand years ago," Jim told me, "after about three hundred years of the right conditions—a cooling climate, expansion of forests."

In the 1800s, salmon ran up the rivers of the Columbia River basin in legendary numbers, an estimated 10 to 16 million each year. The lower basin had runs of all five salmon species, plus steelhead. The mid- and upper basin had runs of chinook, coho, and sockeye salmon, plus steelhead. The Columbia Basin supported what is now thought to have been the largest chinook salmon and steelhead populations in the world, surpassing Alaskan, Canadian, and Asian runs for these species. Without a doubt, the Columbia River had completely recovered from the Ice Age.

Ice ages and volcanic eruptions are catastrophic events. When scientists began studying how river ecosystems respond to disturbance, they looked at all disruptions as catastrophes. Only in the last twenty to thirty years have they begun to differentiate between types of disturbances and to understand the essential roles that some events, like floods and landslides, have in healthy river ecosystems. The disturbance-refugia-recolonization process goes on all the time in rivers at many scales, from a mayfly nymph clinging to the underside of a rock, protected from hungry trout, to an ice-free river where salmon and insects can survive an ice age. To fully understand healthy rivers, I need to understand the complex links between disturbance and life—how algae depend on floods, fish depend on landslides, and rivers need all of these things: the algae, the fish, the floods, and the landslides.

THE CHIWAWA RIVER

The Chiwawa River flows into the Wenatchee River in the North Cascades of Washington, on the east side of the range. It's mid-September, and the road is wet from rain. The wind has bunched the dark gray clouds together, exposing brilliant blue sky. I stop at the Lake Wenatchee Ranger Station, which overlooks log cabins and cedar homes mixed in with the forest along the north shore of Lake Wenatchee. Browsing among the field guides and Smokey Bear T-shirts for sale in the ranger station lobby, I find the free brochures. I pick up an attractive one for the Chiwawa Valley Auto Tour, which guides me up Road 62, a short distance from Lake Wenatchee.

Road 62 is paved partway, then turns into a one-lane road with hard-packed dirt. The Chiwawa Valley, while not wilderness, is almost pristine. Hardly any logging has occurred in the watershed. Some copper, silver, and gold mining went on earlier this century in the upper end of the valley, but the biggest mine, the Red Mountain Development Company, went bankrupt in 1931. The valley bottom is undeveloped except for the single one-lane road I'm traveling on, with some Forest Service campgrounds and trailheads scattered alongside it. The upper Chiwawa watershed is in the half-million-acre Glacier Peak Wilderness.

The blue-green Chiwawa River winds through a dense forest of true firs and Englemann spruce. The thick branches of the true firs form perfectly tapered spires, unlike the lankier Douglas-firs I'm used to. The river's many sloughs, side channels, and point bars are marked by the lighter greens of willows, cottonwoods, and ash trees in the dark green

The healthy Chiwawa River is tightly connected to its watershed, and interacts with the forest, gravel bar, and logjam. (Val Rapp)

fir and spruce forest. The Chiwawa loops and meanders freely through the almost untouched valley. Huge logjams span the whole river and pile up in side channels. I get out and explore one perfectly shaped oxbow curve. The river pinches a big logjam between the bends of its channel, deflecting off the upstream side of the jam and coming all the way around to flow against the downstream side of the logs before winding into another meander. On the upper end of the oxbow, a sandy bar extends into the river.

A healthy river is not only difficult to walk with its dense underbrush, sloughs, and logjams, it's also hard to photograph, because too many trees get in the way. Trying to find a spot where I can get this whole bend in one picture, I come across a cottonwood snag six feet in diameter. The trunk is scarred by old marks of beaver chewing. Apparently the beavers finally gave up on felling the tree, but by then they had girdled it and created a snag.

There's something particular I want to see in the Chiwawa—how a healthy river deals with a major flood. This part of Washington had a big flood in 1990, and I could still see evidence of it earlier in the day as I drove up along the Wenatchee River. In Tumwater Canyon, small driftwood logs had been left behind on granite outcroppings ten feet above the present river level. Below Lake Wenatchee, scoured banks were visible on both sides of the river.

But here along the Chiwawa, I can't even tell there was a recent major flood. This healthy river digested it. The high waters must have flattened the dense riverside underbrush, battering it with logs carried in the current, but I see only a few small spots where the banks were pared away. The riparian forest held the earth in place with a deep network of tree roots, and the underbrush added an insulating layer of protection to the ground. The stands of young willows along some of the sandy beaches and gravel bars look as if they are about six years old; these spots were probably scrubbed clean by the 1990 flood. Along other side channels and curves, I see clumps of trees of various ages. The stand age probably marks the date of the last inundation to reshape that particular spot.

The Chiwawa's logjams are so frequent and so large that they would have slowed and redirected the surging current, causing it to dig out pools, flow into side channels and sloughs, and slow down as it was forced over and through complex accumulations of wood. Some logs must have moved, but they would have traveled only a little ways before getting caught by another jam. The flood reshaped and added to the river's complex structure. It wasn't destructive.

But at one spot, I can see a big scar left by the 1990 flood: a debris flow track down a small stream course. Like Eskimos with their forty words for snow, geotechnical specialists in the dynamic Pacific Northwest landscape have dozens of words for the various ways that the mountainsides collapse, slide, and slump to the valley floors below. I've mastered only one basic distinction: Landslides are moving masses of earth and rock sliding downhill, and they start on the mountain slope outside a stream channel. Debris flows and debris torrents are fast-moving slurries of earth, rock, and water that pour down the small, headwater stream channels on steep slopes. Technically, a debris flow begins in a stream, and a debris torrent occurs when a landslide enters a stream, then mixes with the water and continues down the channel. Everything mixed with the dirt, rock, and water is called debris, regardless of what it was—a large tree, a living salamander, a rotten log, a fern—when the debris flow picked it up.

During the 1990 flood, when the soil on this mountain slope was oversaturated with water, it gave way, and the debris flow chiseled the creek down to bedrock. When the debris flow hit the valley floor, it spread out

In a healthy, resilient river like the Chiwawa, floods and occasional landslides add to the complexity and diversity of the habitat. (Val Rapp)

and created a fan-shaped clearing, then filled it with knocked-down trees, boulders, and mud. Six years later, the stream channel on the mountain slope is still bare, but the alluvial fan has healed considerably. Grasses, shrubs, ponderosa pines, and true firs are starting to grow in the opening. The Forest Service planted the pines, but the rest of the new growth is natural.

A Forest Service stream survey found that the 1990 flood was a positive event for the Chiwawa River. The torrent dug out large new pools, and the debris flows brought wood and boulders, the raw ingredients of river structure, into the river channel. The report does not hint at the beauty and aliveness of the river I'm seeing today, but it summarizes in scientific terms the effects of the 1990 flood on the healthy Chiwawa River:

> *The interaction of the flood with the Chiwawa's large, intact riparian floodplain greatly increased channel complexity. . . . This finding suggests that unmanaged systems with intact, fully*

functional floodplains were further enhanced by the interaction with large flood events, which are a key to shaping and maintaining high-quality fish habitat.

SURVIVAL

Two types of natural disturbances affect river systems: press and pulse. Press disturbances, such as an ice age, change rivers in fundamental ways over long periods of time. It can take a river anywhere from decades to thousands of years to recover after a press disturbance, because streams are sterile, structure is gone, normal river processes have been disrupted, and plants and animals have to travel from refugia a long way away.

Pulse disturbances, such as floods and landslides, last only a short time—they pulse through the river system. Healthy rivers usually recover quickly after pulse disturbances, because their structures and processes are mostly intact, and plants and animals survive the short-lived event in many refugia.

Originally, scientists developed their ideas about stream ecology by studying streams at low flow—the condition streams are in 90 to 95 percent of the time. They didn't see the importance of floods because they dismissed high flows as damaging aberrations. But once researchers looked at floods, the idea of rivers as steady-state systems in which change was slow and gentle fell apart.

Once or twice a year, a naturally flowing river reaches the top of its banks—the annual flood. Occasionally, a river goes over its banks and onto its floodplain. What we call a ten-year flood is a flood that has a one out of ten chance of occurring in any given year, or a 10 percent chance each year. A hundred-year flood has a 1 percent chance of occurring each year, but it could happen twice in five years, or not for a hundred and fifty years.

The hydrologists found that rivers build and maintain their channels through floods. During floods, rivers cut new channels and resculpt older ones, clean silt out of spawning gravels, and flush accumulated leaves and wood into the water from the floodplain. Floodwater soaks into the floodplains and releases slowly, replenishing wetlands and keeping the river flow higher in the summer, months after the high water has subsided. Rivers build their complex pattern of habitats through floods. In the mountains, debris flows scour headwater creeks but bring the building blocks of structure down into streams on valley floors. Like a sloppy cookie dough full of raisins, nuts, and chocolate chips, debris flows in healthy watersheds are chunky with boulders, trees, and gravel mixed into the mud.

The plants and animals of the river have many strategies for surviving in a dynamic environment that includes occasional floods. Here, the same spot on the McKenzie River is shown during winter high water and summer low flow. (Val Rapp)

WHAT THE RIVER REVEALS

The biologists found that, once again, the physical and biological systems of rivers are elegantly connected. Floods wash organic material off the floodplain and into the river and scrub the long strings of filamentous green algae off the riverbed. Afterward, the population of free-floating diatoms and blue-green algae explodes and, along with the new organic debris, fuels a growth spurt all the way up the food chain. Some fish and other fragile bits of flesh are killed in the swirling brown floodwaters and tumbling rocks, but many find safety in side channels and logjams and multiply on the abundance of food and new spawning gravels produced by the flood. From diatoms and caddisfly larvae to salmon and osprey, the life of the river thrives in this dynamic mosaic of shifting patches. Disturbances are change at its worst and best: destructive, chaotic, shattering—and renewing, healing, restorative.

Life meets change and surprise with resilience. But resilience is not just being gutsy. Resilience comes from having strategies for survival. Salmon are the most studied animals of Pacific Northwest rivers, and the most is known about their strategies for survival.

The Pacific Northwest has only seven species of oceangoing salmonids: five species of salmon, one of steelhead, and some sea-run cutthroat trout. That's not many species for a region of such varied habitats. The Dungeness River area on the east side of the Olympic Peninsula, for example, gets only 16 inches of rain a year, whereas a few miles away, the Hoh Valley and other westside river valleys receive an annual 145 inches. Salmon spawn in high-elevation streams and lakes deep in the Idaho mountains, in low-elevation streams a few miles from the ocean, in rivers that flow through high desert, and in rivers that run through forests. The latter vary from coastal rain forests of Sitka spruce and cedar to inland pine forests. The environments are wildly different.

Instead of evolving into many species, salmon have expressed their genetic diversity through hundreds of stocks in a handful of species. Stocks are subpopulations within a species that spawn in a particular river system during a particular season and generally do not interbreed with other stocks. The development of stocks is made possible by two characteristics. The first is salmon's homing instinct to their birth streams, which partially isolates each population of salmon from other stocks. The second is salmon's remarkable degree of genetic plasticity, which enables them to adapt, over a number of generations, to the many different conditions they find in the tumultuous and rigorous environments of Pacific Northwest rivers. So there are Dungeness River pink salmon, Hoh River spring chinook, Salmon River summer steelhead, Tillamook River fall chinook, John Day River summer steelhead, and hundreds of other stocks, each adapted to the unique set of conditions found in their home watershed.

The salmon stocks adapt through variations in such factors as life history, resistance to disease, size, and migratory behavior. In the Sixes River in southwest Oregon, a relatively short river that flows directly into the ocean, chinook salmon have developed five distinct histories varying the amount of time the young fish spend in headwater streams, the river mainstem, and the river estuary before heading out into the ocean. Oregon coastal chinook stocks have different migration patterns in the ocean, with some migrating north toward the Gulf of Alaska and others heading south. The salmon and steelhead of the Columbia River basin once had hundreds of life history variations, such as differences in the length of time spent in freshwater streams, timing of downstream migration, time spent in the estuary, number of years spent at sea before returning to spawn, and spawning habitat. The Dungeness River, which has only seventeen miles accessible to salmon, has two stocks of pinks, one that spawns upriver early in the year, an unusual life history for this species, and one that spawns in the lower river later in the year.

Salmon gamble, but they also hedge their bets. They migrate thousands of miles in their lifetimes through a string of changing environments and a gauntlet of hazards, but the females produce large numbers of eggs. Female chinook salmon may produce from two thousand to seventeen thousand eggs each, with different stocks having different levels. Some life history variations occur within stocks. Most McKenzie River spring chinook return home after four years, but a few return at three years or five, a strategy that protects the run against catastrophes in any single year.

Salmon's loyalty to home is strong, but not total. Almost all return to their birth streams, but every year a few stray to different ones. The strays reinhabit rivers where stocks may have declined or disappeared because of an ice age, a lava flow, or a landslide, and they also ensure that some genetic exchange occurs between stocks. When a river is devastated, such as the Cowlitz was after the eruption of Mount Saint Helens, salmon's flexibility in homing allows them to seek out the nearest river that offers suitable habitat.

A salmon species is like a finely woven, multicolored blanket spread across a landscape. The stocks make up the blanket's colors and patterns. Each stock is unique, but they are all partially interconnected. When a natural catastrophe tears a hole in the fabric, closely related stocks from nearby rivers slowly repair the hole. A few strays darn the first few threads over the gap, and over generations the new run weaves the threads back more and more thickly until the repair is complete. If a severe flood destroys all the eggs one year in a particular river, the variant salmon darn the missing year back into the seamless fabric. The larger the tear, the greater the distance the salmon have to travel to cross it, and the longer it takes to fill in across the hole. The blanket is self-repairing as long as the salmon have strongholds from which they can begin again.

We don't know nearly as much about other river life. Scientists are beginning to find locally adapted populations among fish as different and as ordinary as cutthroat trout, speckled dace, and suckers. These fish do not have the tremendous migratory range of salmon, however, and may take much longer to recolonize rivers. Fish that spend their entire lives in freshwater may not be able to get from one basin to another as easily as salmon, which can travel to another basin by way of the ocean. Even less is known about insects, amphibians, mollusks, and all the other organisms that we tend to overlook but which are part of a healthy river. Scientists studying river recovery after the Mount Saint Helens eruption think it may take decades for an amphibian such as the tailed frog to repopulate all the streams in the blast zone. Disturbances come in many forms and intensities, and life responds with a diversity of survival strategies, life histories, hiding places, and abilities to adapt.

A river is not an organism, but rivers also survive through resilience. A healthy river is self-sustaining and self-healing. It flows with life and energy as well as water. The river pulses with change and response in a dynamic equilibrium. When disruption and damage occur, healing begins from the refugia and spreads out. A healthy river is a self-healing fabric woven of the threads of salmon, stonefly, snail, salamander, and thousands of others.

Scientific articles often include diagrams to illustrate their definitions of healthy rivers. It must seem simple enough when the author starts one of these diagrams. Water flows downstream, and leaves and wood are carried along with it. But the stuff flowing downstream gets caught in nodes like logjams, and there are spirals and knots within the downstream flow. There's more stuff coming in from the sides—trees and boulders from a debris flow, water from last winter's flood filtering through a wetland. Stuff even comes in from underneath, with upwellings and downwellings of water. Then there are the feedback loops, such as adult fish and insects migrating upstream and animals adapting to the river's unique conditions. Inevitably, these diagrams end up with arrows going all over the place—up, down, and sideways, plus curved ones showing feedback loops and crisscrossing ones showing relationships. When I look at these diagrams, I see circles layered over circles. The two-dimensional diagrams are inadequate. A picture of a healthy river needs to be a three-dimensional model of interlocking circles and loops set in motion.

Compare this imaginary, three-dimensional, dynamic model with a flow chart of a human-designed system for producing and transporting something—let's say, the system of Columbia River dams and the connected power grid, a system for producing water and electric power. The flow chart would be complicated, but two dimensions would be adequate. The human-designed system is intricate, but the interrelationships are finite. Some limited feedback and adjustments occur within the system, but most flows are one-way. The system is certainly not self-repairing. The natural river ecosystem, on the other hand, has a near-infinite number of connections, relationships, and feedback loops.

When we say what a healthy river is, we are wise to show some humility. We are just beginning to know rivers. Gordon Reeves, a Forest Service research biologist, told me, "We're scratching the surface with our research—we're moving away from a static view to a more dynamic perspective. We're in our infancy in stream research. The question is, will society be willing to make the changes needed?"

Jim Lichatowich, a fisheries consultant, said, "We don't know what makes a healthy river. We have ideas about what makes healthy rivers. We don't know enough to control and manipulate nature."

Chapter 4

Respect and Transformation

We don't know what we've done to our rivers because we don't know the history of our landscape. For most of us, that knowledge is limited to our personal memories—the history of a lifetime, or even less since so many of us moved to the Pacific Northwest from somewhere else. My memory of this region dates back to 1977; for others, the memories go back only to the 1980s or 1990s.

Rural people are perhaps more likely to have a family history of several generations in one place, such as a ranch. They may know from grandparents what their rivers looked like fifty years ago. But the rivers and river valleys of the Pacific Northwest were changed radically in the 1800s. They have been altered for so long and so thoroughly that the differences are well outside our personal or family memories. An ecologist from a federal agency told me, "People in rural areas think their streams look the way streams should look. To me, they look degraded, but to locals, they look fine."

A history of our landscape could begin millions of years ago, but I will begin with the river ecosystems that developed after the end of the Ice Age ten thousand years ago. By roughly four thousand years ago, the rivers had become like the ones Lewis and Clark saw in 1805, similar to what we can see today in our healthiest, most pristine rivers.

SUSTENANCE

Native Americans have lived in the Pacific Northwest for at least ten thousand years. New archaeological evidence may push that date back even farther. The Indian nations of the Pacific Northwest have distinctive cultures, but there are also some broad similarities. They were hunters, fishers, and gatherers, but they did not just spontaneously collect food from a naturally abundant environment. The Native Americans actively managed the landscape and regulated their harvest of key resources—such as salmon—through a complicated web of customs, actions, and rituals. Their management shaped the land in subtle ways, so subtle that the European-American culture has often failed to notice.

Native American cultures evolved over time, and there is much we do not know. But we do know that over at least the last couple of thousand years, Native Americans in most parts of the Pacific Northwest depended heavily on food resources from rivers. Most Columbia Basin tribes and many coastal societies relied on salmon as a staple food that may have supplied 30 to 40 percent of their total calories. The Columbia River ecosystem supported an estimated fifty thousand Native Americans, who caught as many as 5 million salmon out of the 10 to 16 million that returned up the Columbia each year.

The tribes did most of their fishing at waterfalls, where the salmon had to leap to clear the heights, or at major rapids, where the white water made it harder for the fish to detect nets. Important fishing sites on the Columbia included Kettle Falls in northern Washington, Priest Rapids, Celilo Falls, and the Cascades of the Columbia.

The most famous of these spots was Celilo Falls, at the upper end of the Columbia Gorge. Here the river dropped into a narrow canyon and broke into several channels divided by small islands and rock outcroppings. The Native American fishermen built scaffolding on the rocky promontories and used dipnets and spears to catch the migrating salmon navigating the narrow chutes of churning water and falls. The fishing village was also the center of a huge trade fair every summer. Celilo Falls continued to be an important Native American fishing site until it was drowned in the reservoir rising behind The Dalles Dam in 1956.

The fishing at Celilo Falls was on a seasonal cycle. It began when spring chinook arrived at the end of April, after the First Salmon ceremony opened salmon fishing for the year. Later in May, when spring runoff poured into the Columbia from melting snow in the Rockies, the river rose and flooded the rocky points. The tribes took a break from fishing and moved to the camas meadows to harvest camas bulbs and other roots. By late June or early July, the river level had dropped, and the fishermen returned to catch sockeye, chinook, and summer steelhead. In late summer, the Native Americans traveled to the high mountain meadows for huckleberries, coming back once again to the river for the last fishing season of the year, the fall runs of chinook in September and October.

Fishing at Celilo Falls was carefully regulated. The site was governed by a salmon chief who was distinct from the village chief. The salmon chief opened and closed fishing at the site seasonally and also on a daily basis. The closures allowed salmon to escape the harvest, ensuring that enough spawned to perpetuate future runs. Dozens of rocky points and islands at the falls had names, and the use of each spot was controlled by a specific family.

Salmon were not the only food harvested from the rivers. The Native Americans of the Columbia Basin collected freshwater mussels, which were large and plentiful. The Columbia tribes also caught large-scale and bridge-lip suckers in the tributary streams where they spawned from late February into March. In the Klamath Lake area, where there were many large, shallow lakes and extensive wetlands, the Klamath Indians fished for the Lost River sucker and the shortnose sucker when they migrated up spawning rivers that fed into the lake. The Klamath tribes also hunted the ducks and geese that used the extensive wetlands and collected water lily seeds.

Salmon runs were not as large in the Willamette River basin as in the main Columbia Basin, mainly because of the natural barrier of Willamette Falls on the lower river, near present-day Oregon City. The Native Americans of the Willamette Valley caught some salmon but also relied on many other foods, such as camas bulbs and game. The tribes burned the valley grasslands regularly, deliberately maintaining the prairie and savanna landscape needed by the plants and animals the people depended on. Some of the fires carried into the forests in the mountain ranges bordering the valley and were an important force in shaping the patterns of disturbances affecting the rivers.

Native Americans used the natural resources for subsistence—physical survival—and for sustenance—spiritual survival. The archaeological record shows that some tribes probably overfished some salmon runs, causing the temporary collapse of those stocks. But the Native American management system had a direct feedback loop since overharvest led fairly quickly to a serious gap in their yearly food supply. They learned that they must treat the salmon with respect or else the salmon would stop coming back each year. The Native Americans showed their respect for salmon in many ways, including the First Salmon ceremony each spring, fishing customs and regulations, proper ways of cooking salmon, and careful disposal of the remains. Showing respect for salmon was not only a way to have enough to eat; it was also a way to understand human responsibilities in the world and to appreciate the generosity of nature.

PRODUCTION

European-Americans reached the Pacific Northwest in the late 1700s, first as visitors and then to stay. They, too, used the region's natural abundance for subsistence, but they also used its resources for production. From the first Spanish and American fur traders to visit the coastline, the goal of these new peoples was to ship products to other geographical areas—the East Coast, China, Europe, and later the booming mine towns of California—and to create wealth. At first the money flowed to companies and investors headquartered in those distant regions, such as the Hudson's Bay Company, John Jacob Astor, and Boston investors. Eventually, as cities grew in the Pacific Northwest, some of the profits flowed to local companies and investors. The Native Americans had trading networks, but the European-Americans went beyond simple trade. They wanted fortunes.

Beavers, salmon, trees, and ultimately even the water itself were seen as commodities, no different from a rifle or a dress or a frying pan produced in a factory and sold for a profit. Natural resources were there to be bought, sold, and controlled, with no intrinsic or spiritual value. The European-Americans didn't think about what the salmon might need to keep coming back every year, or what the rivers might need to keep being homes for salmon.

The new people learned the region by traveling its rivers, first upstream from the ocean, then downstream on overland expeditions. From the 1770s to the 1790s, ships from Spain, Great Britain, the United States, and Russia visited the Pacific Northwest, mapping out such major features as Puget Sound and the Columbia River and trading with the coastal and lower Columbia River Indians for furs.

A wave of smallpox swept through Native American communities about 1775, brought by one of the fur-trading ships. A second smallpox epidemic ravaged tribes along the Columbia in 1801. Historians estimate that these two epidemics had cut the Native American population in half by the time Lewis and Clark came down the Snake and Columbia Rivers in 1805.

Lewis and Clark and their small expedition were the first white men to travel overland through present-day Idaho, Washington, and Oregon, although some Hudson's Bay Company explorers had reached the Pacific coast farther north a few years earlier. Lewis and Clark's detailed expedition journals were the first written descriptions of the region's Native American peoples and landscape. However, the British and American fur traders who had visited the coast earlier had already made a considerable impact by promoting excessive trapping and by inadvertently introducing smallpox. Thus in 1805, Lewis and Clark were already too late to see a culture and a region unchanged by European-Americans.

The fur trade dominated the regional economy from the 1780s to the late 1840s. Sea otters were overtrapped by 1812, and beaver was the main fur in demand after that. The British Hudson's Bay Company controlled the area that is now Oregon and Washington, and American "mountain men" did most of the trapping in the Rockies. Instead of trading with Native Americans, the mountain men trapped all year, then once a year brought their furs to trading posts or rendezvous—big gatherings where buyers and trappers met and did business, mixed in with a lot of drinking, carousing, and storytelling. The Hudson's Bay Company pursued a deliberate policy of trapping beaver completely out of the Snake River area in order to create a "fur desert" that would keep the mountain men from moving farther west. By the late 1840s, overtrapping and changing fashions had created a collapse in the fur trade.

Although there was no deliberate policy to destroy the Native Americans, the European-Americans continued to inadvertently spread diseases to which the native peoples had no resistance. An epidemic in 1824–25 was probably smallpox. The worst epidemic lasted from 1830 to 1833 and was probably malaria, possibly brought by a trading ship from Mexico. The outbreak flared every summer for four years, killing an estimated 90 percent of the Native Americans living along the lower Columbia River and in the Willamette Valley. The Indian cultures of these areas were essentially destroyed. Few adults were left to teach the traditions, religion, and lifeways to the surviving children. Farther inland, Oregon Trail travelers brought measles, respiratory infections, whooping cough, and other diseases that killed and weakened many Native Americans in those areas.

With the Native American population decimated, European-Americans rapidly became the dominant culture in the Pacific Northwest. The surviving tribes protected their access to resources as best they could in negotiations with the settlers. In many treaties, Native Americans reserved the right to fish, hunt, and collect berries at "usual and accustomed" places, protecting their fishing privileges at Celilo Falls and other locations. But they lost any voice in the regulation of resources and did not regain a significant role in salmon management until the 1970s, when they pursued lawsuits over their treaty fishing claims. Beginning in 1974, a series of federal court decisions protected Native American fishing rights and restored some Native American power in salmon and river administration.

By the mid-1840s, a white population of just five thousand Americans and a smaller number of British settlers had made changes that would have a significant impact on the future. The loss of so many Native Americans put an end to prairie burning and a regulated subsistence fishery, and the fur trappers brought beaver to the edge of extinction. Beavers were a keystone species in stream ecosystems. Their stick-and-mud dams created complex habitats of small ponds and backwaters that were refugia for smaller fish during winter floods. The small dams slowed floodwater and spread it out, allowing it to soak in and release slowly back into the stream over the hot, dry summers, like a sponge slowly drying out. The loss of beaver dams and ponds led to lower water tables along riparian corridors and fewer refugia for overwintering juvenile salmon, and left streams more susceptible to being downcut by floods.

Enterprises had been started that would lead to major industries. By 1823, the Hudson's Bay Company was packing salmon with salt at Fort George, near Astoria, and shipping them out of the region. In 1827, the company built the first sawmill in the Pacific Northwest, near Fort Vancouver, across the Columbia from present-day Portland. The Whitmans and Spaldings, Protestant missionaries, were diverting river water through irrigation ditches at their respective missions in eastern Washington and western Idaho. In 1846, farmers in the territory of Oregon produced more than 160,000 bushels of wheat.

Despite these changes, in the mid-1840s, Pacific Northwest rivers were still very close to pristine. They were tightly connected to their floodplains through multiple channels; dense forests of cottonwoods, alders, Oregon ash, and conifers; and extensive wetlands and sloughs. The lower rivers were biological hotspots, the most productive part of the stream network. Salmon and steelhead runs migrated up Pacific coast rivers from the San Diego River in southern California to Alaska. Dozens of species and distinctive subspecies of minnows, chubs, suckers, sculpins, and trout swam in the streams and lakes. Rivers and wetlands were crowded with ducks, bald eagles, osprey, and other birds.

Fires and floods were the most common large disturbances. Big forest fires in the mountains burned thousands of acres and left slopes of black snags and scorched soils that led to frequent landslides in the deforested areas for years afterward. Floods rolled down river valleys from time to time, lifting and rearranging the logjams and resculpting the channels. The rivers had a deep capacity to absorb these events and digested floods and fires as they had thousands of times before in their long, richly textured existence. A watershed burned over by a large fire had refugia—springbrooks, deep pools, and patches of moist riparian forest only singed by the flames. The blackened watershed took decades to recover completely, but it was surrounded by intact watersheds that were sources of new life that flew or swam or walked to the recovering river. Rivers knew how to restore themselves.

At that moment, in the 1840s, the trickle of settlers was about to turn into a torrent. The rivers were about to be transformed by forces unlike any they had ever experienced. The 1840s were not the end for wild, healthy rivers in the Pacific Northwest. But those years were the end of the beginning.

The first big wagon trains journeyed over the Oregon Trail in 1843, bringing eight hundred to nine hundred new settlers to the Northwest that year. For the next several decades, each spring a wave of travelers started out in Missouri and rolled west, arriving in the Oregon Country in late summer through fall. Once this influx of pioneers had begun, change came quickly to the Pacific Northwest.

Fifty years of western gold rushes began with the discovery of gold in California in 1848. In 1852, the discovery of gold near present-day Jacksonville in southern Oregon set off the first gold rush in the Pacific Northwest. It was followed by others—at Fort Colville in northeastern Washington, in the Blue Mountains in eastern Oregon, and in the Idaho mountains. A small gold rush took place up the valley of the Blue River, a tributary of the McKenzie, in the 1860s, and again around the turn of the century.

Gold nuggets and flakes had eroded from mountain canyons and washed into river gravels that had accumulated over thousands of years. Panning did relatively little damage to the rivers, but it was quickly replaced by placer and hydraulic mining, techniques that used water cannons, sluice boxes, and other devices to move tons of earth and rock. The equipment dug down into the alluvial deposits, churning up gravel bars, riverbanks, and riverbeds. Rocks and sand spewed out the other end of the machines and were left in heaps along one or both edges of a river. The larger boulders were often stacked on the piles last, covering the smaller material and creating heavily armored mounds that the current could not break down.

While the mining was going on, the water ran muddy for months at a time, and the silt smothered aquatic life for a long way downstream. After the miners had worked through a stretch, the waterway flowed on bedrock at the bottom of a deeply incised channel, looking more like a sorry example of a drainage ditch than a river. The mined stream course was washed clean of the thousands of insect nymphs, juvenile fish, snails, and salamanders that had once inhabited it.

Hardrock mining, which meant digging tunnels into mountainsides, required a lot of investment money and started more slowly. Gold was discovered in the Coeur d'Alene region of Idaho in 1884, and here the miners found lodes of gold and silver that required deep tunnels. Gold refineries and silver smelters were needed to extract pure metals from the ore-bearing rock. Lead and zinc mining soon followed. The wastewater, carrying lead, zinc, cadmium, and mercury, poured into streams and eventually flowed into Coeur d'Alene Lake.

The first California gold rush suddenly provided a market for farmers in Oregon, which was remote from eastern markets in this era before transcontinental railroads. The other gold rushes that followed offered additional markets and fueled the early growth of Northwest agriculture, which went quickly from self-sufficient homesteads to an agricultural industry that exported wheat, beef, lambs, and wool. Agriculture developed first in the Willamette Valley. By the 1850s, when the most desirable valley land was already claimed, settlers began to clear the dense forests near the rivers, close off side channels and sloughs, and farm floodplains that were occasionally inundated.

Most of the Pacific Northwest was in the dry interior east of the Cascade Mountains. Although much snow fell in the interior mountain ranges and the runoff created large rivers like the Columbia and the Snake, the valleys and plateaus suitable for farming got little rain. Settlement was slower in the interior, but these arid lands were also rich in resources.

The grasslands of the high plateaus of eastern Washington and Oregon soon attracted cattlemen and sheepmen with their herds and flocks. The native grasses had evolved under the light grazing of deer and antelope and did not grow back well under the heavier grazing pressure of cattle and sheep. Sagebrush and cheatgrass, which were not palatable to livestock, became more prominent on the open range. Cattle and sheep clustered on stream bottoms in the dry country, drawn to the water, shade, and lush grasses. In some cases, the livestock overgrazed riparian areas and trampled banks. Beavers had been particularly important in the eastside streams. Their ponds slowed down the spring runoff when the snow melted and allowed water to soak into the ground, raising the water table. Later, during the hot, dry summer, the stream flow stayed higher, and the riparian corridor supported more grasses and shrubs. With beavers scarce, some streams turned to trickles by late summer.

Basically, there were two solutions to agriculture in the dry interior: dryland farming and irrigation farming. Dryland farming techniques were worked out in the Walla Walla Valley of eastern Washington in the 1860s, and wheat farming became a major industry in southeastern Washington.

Irrigation developed slowly at first in the Pacific Northwest. Many rivers were in canyons below the plateaus. In the 1800s there was no way to pump water up out of the deep canyons, limiting the areas where irrigation was feasible. Irrigation projects in the nineteenth century were built by individual farmers, private companies, or farm communities, and many attempts failed to be profitable. Early irrigation systems simply

Hydraulic gold mining destroyed riverbeds and banks and flushed enormous sediment loads downstream (Sterling Hydraulic Mine, Oregon). (photo courtesy Oregon Historical Society, OrHi 65160)

diverted water from streams. Later, more elaborate systems were built that included networks of ditches and canals, dams across smaller streams and rivers, and reservoirs.

Mormon farmers moved into southeastern Idaho beginning in 1855. They had developed irrigation expertise in Utah, and they worked together as a community. The first Mormon settlement was abandoned in 1858, but others had greater success. Over time the Mormons developed communities and irrigated farms around Bear Lake and Franklin in southern Idaho. Other farmers began irrigation withdrawals in the mid-Columbia region in the 1850s.

Compared with the reclamation projects of the twentieth century, nineteenth-century irrigation projects were small, but they had a significant impact on some rivers. Generally, no attempt was made to screen irrigation diversions. Millions of juvenile salmon migrating to the ocean were transported from the river right along with the water and ended their short lives in apple orchards or watermelon fields. Even as early as 1890, fish commissioners had made repeated calls to stop the loss of juvenile salmon through irrigation systems, but their requests were ignored. Although dam building was limited by the engineering capability of the time and available investment capital, dams were raised across some streams and smaller rivers, but without fish passage. There were no limits on how much water could be withdrawn from rivers, and some were drained almost dry during peak watering times in summer months. The Umatilla was already overappropriated by 1904, with more demand for water in late summer than the river could supply.

In the mid-1800s, people still knew the Pacific Northwest by rivers. Overland travel was difficult and limited to wagon routes, which usually followed river valleys as much as possible. Water travel was just as difficult on the meandering rivers with their multiple channels, waterfalls, rapids, and logjams. The complicated patterns of upstream and downstream flow that worked so well for river ecosystems were not what people wanted—they wanted to travel faster. "Streamlined," in this case, meant literally making streams more like straight lines instead of knotted, braided ropes entangled with the countryside.

The first steamboat in the Pacific Northwest was the *Beaver*, delivered to the Hudson's Bay Company at Fort Vancouver in 1836. The *Columbia* was the first to offer regular service between Astoria and Portland, beginning in 1850. Other steamships quickly followed on the Columbia and lower Willamette Rivers. Gold rushes in the interior provided the impetus for building steam vessels to operate on large inland rivers, such as the Snake, and larger lakes, such as Coeur d'Alene. At waterfalls and major rapids, like the Cascades and Celilo Falls on the Columbia, steamboat companies had to build short roads to portage passengers and freight around the barrier, then transfer them to another ship on the next stretch of river. However, even with the portages, steamboats made traveling faster and easier.

River navigability had to be improved to accommodate the new steamships. The rivers were full of driftwood logs that could snag a boat or puncture its hull. Old waterlogged snags drifted below the surface or had one end stuck in the river bottom. Other logs were piled up in logjams or wedged against one bank and extended out into the river. One of the U.S. Army Corps of Engineers' first responsibilities in the Pacific Northwest was snagging, or pulling out the driftwood logs, and channelizing rivers to improve navigation.

In the 1860s, the Willamette River between Harrisburg and Eugene had four or five main channels in most reaches. By 1872, crews were channelizing the river—working to confine it to one deeper passage by closing off the channels and sloughs with small dams, built with snags pulled from the water and trees cut from the banks. Because of its multiple courses, this 15-mile stretch of the Willamette had 150 miles of shoreline before channelization began. By 1910, the same stretch had only 72 miles of shoreline, less than half as much.

The Corps of Engineers also removed thousands of snags from the Willamette and other Pacific Northwest rivers to make the waterways safe for steamboats. Sample statistics from the Corps' annual reports show that along 170 miles of the Willamette River, work crews took out 1,566 snags between 1870 and 1875; another 4,620 snags between 1876 and 1880; and 3,900 snags between 1881 and 1885. Thousands of riverbank trees were also cut and hauled away to keep them from falling into the water. Many of the riparian trees were black cottonwoods 6 feet in diameter and a 150 feet tall.

Enormous amounts of wood were extracted from other rivers throughout the region. Driftwood logs were piled deep on the shores of estuaries and at the mouths of rivers, and much of this wood was also carried away. Rivers in the lowlands around Puget Sound, Willamette Valley, and Oregon coastal valleys often had such extensive sloughs and marshes, mixed with logjams, that no obvious main channel existed. Since these areas were settled early, their rivers were often the first to be channelized so that land could be drained for farms and towns and the rivers navigated. Washington's Stillaguamish River, which flows into Puget Sound, had six huge logjams between tidewater and river mile seventeen. These jams held so many trees that it took a crew working from a steam-driven snag boat six months to clear a channel only a hundred feet wide.

Steamboats used ten to thirty cords of wood per day. Trees near the river's edge were the most convenient source, so riparian forests were cut down to fuel ships gliding down the cleared channels of Pacific Northwest rivers.

The steamboats were replaced by railroads after only a few decades, but rivers used for steamship travel had been radically changed. Snagging, riparian tree cutting, and channelization had removed basic food sources, structure, and habitat, greatly reducing the rivers' ability to support life and digest floods. Even after steamboat traffic had declined, the changes were maintained to keep rivers navigable for log rafts and barges.

Railroads made overland travel the dominant mode of transportation in the Pacific Northwest. Local lines were built in the late 1850s, and the first transcontinental railroad to the Northwest (the second in the country) was completed in 1883. The cross-country journey that had taken from three to five months suddenly dropped to five or six days, and migrants poured into the region, particularly into Washington. A rail link was completed to California in 1887, and the regional network expanded rapidly. Railroads made it possible to ship Pacific Northwest lumber, wheat, and other products to national markets at competitive prices for the first time. The network of tracks replaced rivers, trails, and wagon roads with the first true regional transportation grid, a linear system that made travel fast, cheap, and safe.

The development of the railroads was a necessary precursor to the great expansion of the Pacific Northwest's resource industries in the early twentieth century. Timber eventually became the region's trademark industry. By 1851, Portland had a steam-driven sawmill, and Oregon City had five water-powered mills. In 1853, Andrew Jackson Pope and F. C. Talbot picked a mill site on Puget Sound. Until the early 1880s, logging was done mostly near large bays and rivers such as Puget Sound, Grays Harbor, Coos Bay, and the lower Columbia River, since water transport was the only way to move large amounts of timber. Most lumber was exported to San Francisco, the biggest market on the West Coast, but the railroad boom of the late 1800s created a regional market for ties and bridge timbers.

As loggers moved on to new stands of timber, they cut their way up the river valleys of the Pacific Northwest. Logs would be dragged to the river's edge by teams of oxen or sent shooting into the water down flumes. Loggers built splash dams, temporary wooden barriers that turned rivers into short-term millponds. When the backed-up river was filled with logs, the splash dam was released, and a flood of logs and water shot down the channel. Loggers pulled jams apart with horses or blasted them loose with dynamite. These log drives scoured rivers in a way that natural floods never did, scraping them clean of the driftwood accumulations that were an essential part of the river ecosystem. Downstream, the men lashed the logs into rafts and floated them to mills. Later, steam-powered yarders called steam donkeys replaced the oxen and speeded up logging, and the construction of narrow-gauge railroads into the mountains opened up more forests.

The salmon fishing industry was different from any other resource-based enterprise. Salmon were like gifts—every year they came up the rivers of their own accord, showing the amazing generosity that the Native Americans respected so highly. It was as if the old-growth trees had walked over the hills to the mill, or crops had gone to sea as sprouts and returned ripe. Although Native Americans continued their traditional fishing, European-American fishermen rapidly came to dominate commercial salmon fishing. The industry was unregulated for many years, and every man fished as he pleased.

By 1854, Columbia River salmon were being salted at the mouth of the Columbia at Astoria, and at the Cascades, 150 miles upstream, for shipping east. However, it was the invention of canning that exploded the salmon industry into the fishing frenzy of the late nineteenth century. The first salmon cannery in North America was established on a raft in the Sacramento River in 1864 by George W. and William Hume, brothers, and Andrew S. Hapgood, all from Maine. In 1866, they moved their operation to the Columbia. Salmon canneries shot up throughout the Pacific Northwest over the next few years—there were fifty-five on or near the Columbia by 1883, and others on nearly every major coastal river in Oregon. Entrepreneurs did not overlook the huge salmon runs of Puget Sound, and by 1877, canning facilities were spreading along its shores as well.

Astoria was the center of the Columbia canning industry. Canneries were built on pilings at the river's edge, and fish waste was simply thrown into the river, where eventually it drifted offshore. Columbia River fishermen went after salmon with every kind of gear they could devise—gillnets, fish wheels, dipnets, purse seines, and set nets—and in the peak years of the late 1800s, they caught more salmon than the canneries could handle. Tons of dead fish were tossed overboard into the river.

In the early years, fishermen kept only chinook, the largest salmon species, also known as king salmon. The Columbia still had hundred-pound chinook then, that traveled all the way up the river to its upper reaches in Canada. The peak chinook catch on the Columbia was in 1883, with 43 million pounds taken, but by 1890, the kings were declining. Although the total pounds of salmon canned continued to increase for several decades, the fishermen were now bringing in sockeye, coho, chum, and steelhead along with declining amounts of chinook.

In the peak years of the late 1800s, the lower Columbia was jammed with boats. The state of Oregon and the territory of Washington made their first attempts to regulate fishing in the 1870s, by not allowing nets to completely block an entire river and by having weekly and seasonal closures so some fish could escape. Little was known about the biology of salmon or the size of the runs, so these restrictions were only blind

Forests near rivers and bays were the first to be logged in the 1800s. Log drives moved the timber to mills. (photo courtesty Oregon Historical Society, OrHi 59863)

When a splash dam was released, the surge of logs and water often gouged and eroded the river channel (near Albany, 1907). (photo courtesy Lane County Historical Museum, L4F/2032)

attempts to let some escapement occur. However, the rules were widely ignored, and fish commissioners did not have the police it would have taken to enforce them. By the 1890s, the commissioners were warning that the salmon runs were declining because of overfishing, and in fact might be completely destroyed if overfishing continued.

The first salmon hatchery on the Pacific Coast was built in 1872, by the U.S. Fish Commission on the McCloud River in northern California, and the first salmon hatchery in the Pacific Northwest went into operation on Oregon's Clackamas River in 1877. The early hatchery managers knew almost nothing about salmon biology—they didn't know that salmon needed high-protein food and would die on a carbohydrate diet; they didn't know what kinds of diseases salmon might get or how to prevent these illnesses in a crowded hatchery; and they didn't know at what age the fish should be released, or in how many years they would come back. As a result, early hatcheries had extremely poor returns.

However, neither lack of knowledge nor poor results dampened the enthusiasm for fish hatcheries. Hatcheries seemed to promise that salmon could be managed like wheat fields or factory goods. Optimistic fishery managers thought they could eliminate the natural oscillations of wild runs and replace them with predictable crops of hatchery salmon. A human-engineered system would replace the unpredictable and now apparently failing natural system. Fishing levels would not have to be reduced, and if any of the many human activities around streams had happened to damage salmon habitat a little bit, hatcheries would make up for the loss. By 1900, the new state of Washington had fourteen salmon hatcheries, and Oregon had also built additional ones.

By the end of the nineteenth century, the people of the Pacific Northwest no longer knew their region by its rivers. They knew it now by the routes of railroads and the survey lines of property ownership. We tend to think the degradation of our rivers is a product of the twentieth century, when big dams were built, highways were paved, cities exploded, and big companies came to dominate resource industries. But by 1900, the rivers of the Pacific Northwest were already different physically and biologically from what they had been for the previous four thousand years. Most changes had occurred in the lower reaches of rivers—the Columbia below The Dalles, the Willamette from its mouth to Eugene, Puget Sound rivers, Oregon coastal rivers, and the lower stretches of eastside rivers. The rivers would be altered even more in the twentieth century, but the essential transformation had happened—the cultural understanding of rivers and our responsibilities toward them had changed.

THE WILLAMETTE RIVER

Champoeg State Park (pronounced *shampoo-ey*) lies along the Willamette River not quite halfway between Portland and Salem. The road from Wilsonville to the park follows the Willamette. Along the riverfront are large, elegant homes with three-car garages, boat docks, and tasteful landscaping. Small motorboats buzz up and down the river freely. On the other side of the road, away from the river, I see fields of hay, tomatoes, and corn and farmhouses. Inside the park I drive past mowed fields and scattered groves of oaks, ponderosa pines, and Douglas-firs. The strip of forest bordering the river is no more than a hundred feet wide in most places and is composed of cottonwoods, alders, bigleaf maples, and Douglas-firs. Scotch broom, thistle, and English ivy, none of which are native plants, are widespread.

After almost 200 years of development, oxbow lakes and other river-related habitats are now rare along the Pacific Northwest's major rivers. (Val Rapp)

Respect and Transformation

The original town of Champoeg, established in 1852, was on the flat at the top of the thirty-foot riverbank. Most of the buildings were swept away in the flood of 1861, and in 1892 the community was abandoned. I can see that last winter's flood, the flood of '96, just reached the top of the bank, where it left sticks and river debris caught on the upstream side of exposed tree roots. Some small cottonwoods lower on the bank toppled.

After leaving Champoeg, I drive southwest through French Prairie. This area was settled by retired French-Canadian fur trappers from Hudson's Bay Company, who started small farms. French Prairie is an industrial agriculture area now. I drive past fields of hops, green beans, tomatoes, nursery stock, and orchards. Farm workers have harvested some of the hops already, while in other places the vines are still green garlands growing up twelve-foot strings. The nursery stock fields have long rows of young trees and shrubs that will be shipped to landscapers and gardeners. Portable outhouses are scattered here and there among the crops.

Willamette Mission State Park is south of French Prairie. This partially natural area has remnants of the old Willamette—one oxbow lake and one slough, examples of the many lakes and sloughs that used to form a broad band along the river's course. Mission Lake, a narrow crescent bordered by willows and partially covered by water lilies, was formed some time in the past when the Willamette cut straight across the loop of a meander during a flood and left its old channel as a small lake. On one side stands the country's official, national-champion black cottonwood—the largest of its species. It is 158 feet tall and over 8 feet in diameter, making it a giant among broad-leaved trees. The Willamette used to have thousands of trees this size in its riparian forests, shading its thousands of oxbow lakes and sloughs. Now there is one—one tree, one lake, in a state park.

I park my car and walk over to the cottonwood. Grasses and willows edge most of the small lake, but the ground is trampled and dusty in a circle around the trunk of the champion tree. I walk around it too, feeling the rough bark, looking up into the spiral of branches, listening to the leaves rustle in the warm breeze of the September afternoon. I take some pictures, and then return to my car. I want to leave the tree alone.

Chapter 5

Broken Connections

W e learned how to build large dams across large rivers in the early twentieth century. Unfortunately, we thought rivers were only conduits that carried water, and we used brilliant engineering and a lot of concrete to control that flow, generate power, hold back floods, and make the desert bloom. We didn't know rivers as healthy living systems embedded in watersheds.

Rivers are tightly linked to their watersheds, and when links are broken, the damage spreads throughout the river ecosystem in a series of cascading effects. Usually we are busy doing more than one thing in a watershed, and each of our actions leads to another series of cascading effects. It's like throwing stones into a pond. The first stone creates a widening circle of ripples, and the next stone creates another circle. After several stones are tossed, the ripples begin to cross each other and create intricate patterns that could not have been predicted from the original splashes. By then, the person on shore cannot tell which ripple came from which stone.

It's hard to follow the cascading effects through the watershed. But it's easy to pick the event that made the big splash.

THE ELWHA RIVER
The Elwha River on the Olympic Peninsula flows north into the Strait of Juan de Fuca just west of the small city of Port Angeles. The watershed has an area of 321 square miles, 80 percent of it within Olympic National Park. The Elwha is only forty-five miles long, but it has over a hundred miles of tributary streams. It comes down out of the Olympic Mountains through a valley that alternates between deep, narrow gorges and open bottomland. Although the Elwha and its watershed are not very

large by Pacific Northwest standards, it is one of the region's most famous salmon rivers.

The Elwha used to have ten runs of anadromous fish—spring and fall chinook, coho, pink, chum, and sockeye salmon, plus summer and winter steelhead, sea-run cutthroat trout, and sea-run bull trout (also known as Dolly Varden). Many rivers larger than the Elwha have runs of only two or three anadromous fish species. The Elwha S'Klallam Indians used to fish year-round on the Elwha, which was the heart of their culture and economy.

The best-known Elwha salmon was a run of large chinook. These king salmon, which often weighed over a hundred pounds, were the largest

The lower Elwha River looks beautiful, but is starved of fresh supplies of gravel and logs, the raw materials of river habitats, blocked by the dam upstream. (Val Rapp)

WHAT THE RIVER REVEALS

chinook on the Olympic Peninsula, and among the largest anywhere. They probably developed their large size and long life cycle in response to the long, powerful rapids that pounded through the Elwha's narrow canyons. Older, larger fish were more likely to succeed in getting through the rapids to the miles of ideal spawning streams upriver.

Construction began on Elwha Dam in 1910, in a gorge only five miles upstream from the river mouth. Although the state of Washington already had laws requiring dams to provide fishways for migrating fish, the dam's owners, Thomas Aldwell and his Olympic Power and Development Company, did not include any type of fish passage in their design. While crews were blasting and building, the Washington state fish commissioner contacted Aldwell repeatedly about the legal requirement for a fishway, but Aldwell ignored the requests and the state was unable or unwilling to enforce the law.

The partially built dam was a barrier to the migrating fish by 1911. When construction finished in 1913, the dam completely blocked returning salmon from all but the lower five miles of the river. Run after run showed up at the base of the dam and jumped repeatedly, trying to find a way upstream, but they were hopelessly, permanently stopped. The reservoir behind the dam was named Lake Aldwell, in honor of Thomas Aldwell.

The Olympic Power and Development Company finally reached a "compromise" agreement with the state that allowed it to build a fish hatchery at the dam as a replacement for the fish passage, even though state law did not allow for substitutions for the required fishways. The hatchery was unsuccessful, and was abandoned in 1922.

Fifteen years after completion of the Elwha Dam, construction began on a second dam upriver. The Glines Canyon Dam took shape between 1925 and 1927 in another gorge. Fish passage was not an issue since the runs had already been blocked downstream. Crown Zellerbach eventually bought the two dams and used the electricity to run their pulp and paper mill in Port Angeles until 1987, when they sold the dams and power plants to the James River Paper Company. The hydropower is currently used by Daishowa America's pulp and paper mill in Port Angeles, supplying about 38 percent of the mill's energy needs.

I chose to visit the Elwha because it is a classic example of how a river cut in two by dams is degraded both upriver and downriver from the dams. In a morning walk near the Elwha Campground in July, I stop on a bridge that crosses the river below Glines Canyon. Two young raccoons follow their mother along the bank in the shade of alders. The dam is upstream, hidden by the bends of the narrow gorge, but I can see its effects. It not only stopped fish from coming upstream, it blocked the normal downstream flows of sediments and logs, the raw materials of river structure.

The Elwha flows from steep, geologically active mountains and winds through a valley with deep deposits of glacial till. During winter floods the river carries tons of sediment downstream. Protected by the park, the upper watershed is unroaded and unlogged, and all sediment— including cobbles, gravels, sand, and dirt—comes from natural processes. The river dumps its bedload, an estimated 180,000 cubic yards per year, when it hits the slack water of Lake Mills behind Glines Canyon Dam. Since the dam was closed in 1927, about 11.3 million cubic yards of sediment have accumulated in the reservoir. The river downstream is starved of the raw materials that build riverbeds and gravel bars. Instead of the open bars and sandy beaches that I saw on the Hoh and McKenzie Rivers, the Elwha below Glines Canyon Dam is closed in by trees.

Downstream from the bridge, a midriver island is covered by a dense stand of alders, which lean over the water, reaching for sun. I can see the island was a gravel bar once, but there is no exposed gravel any more, and there hasn't been for years, judging by the height of the grove. As far downriver as I can see, trees crowd to the river's edge. I don't see any gravel or sand along the banks, and the smallest rocks are the size of my fist.

For years, both dams were operated only to meet the power needs at the mill, which meant frequent, extreme variations in discharge, completely unlike the river's natural flooding patterns. The high-powered discharges scoured the sand and gravels out of the riverbed, and Glines Canyon Dam kept new sediment out of the system. In the five miles of river still accessible to salmon below Elwha Dam, where remnant salmon runs struggled to survive, the loss of fine gravels ruined the spawning beds and rearing habitat. Abrupt fluctuations in water flow often stranded young and adult fish. The river developed a heavily armored channel lined with larger rocks not easily moved by the current. Amazingly, remnant runs of chinook, chum, and pink salmon, steelhead, and sea-run cutthroat trout are still hanging on in the poor habitat left in the lower river. But the returning fish are counted by the tens or hundreds, and no one has seen a hundred-pound chinook in the Elwha in decades.

Near its mouth, the Elwha used to migrate back and forth across a floodplain over a mile wide. It is now constrained to one channel. The loss of new gravel and sand has affected the landscape beyond the river mouth. The beaches at the mouth of the Elwha have eroded, losing 75 to 150 feet since the dams. The shoreline near the mouth has receded and steepened, and the intertidal zone is now dominated by large cobbles instead of sand. To the east, Ediz Hook, a long, curved sandspit that protects the harbor of Port Angeles, is eroding without new supplies of sand from the river. The Army Corps of Engineers now spends $100,000 a year to control erosion at Ediz Hook, replacing a service the Elwha used to provide for free.

Glines Canyon Dam also prevented fallen trees from drifting downstream. The river below the dams has been starved of new driftwood logs for more than eighty years. I see no logjams or large logs at all in the river channel. Without logjams, the river has gradually lost its deep pools, cover, refugia, and an important substrate for the food chain—from fungi, to insect nymphs, to fish. The river is not dead. But a complex, resilient web has lost many of its threads and linkages and is now reduced to a few strands.

On this bridge, I am just below Glines Canyon Dam, which is the dividing point between the upper, free-flowing river and the lower, dammed river. Below me, the water moves, but the armored channel is unmoving. The once dynamic river is fixed, its potency cut by the dams. Other campers are out walking along the riverbank now, and the raccoons have disappeared. The alders provide a cooling shade, the canyon is overwhelmingly green and close, and the water is a translucent green. I imagine the other campers think how beautiful the river is, while I am thinking sadly how diminished it is.

I spend the afternoon hiking along the upper Elwha, above the dams and roads. Western redcedars and western hemlocks are mixed with the Douglas-fir forest. Groves of bigleaf maples stand on the older river terraces. Alien thistles have invaded this wild valley and grow among the wild grasses. Here I can see everything that was missing below—open gravel bars with new deposits of gravel and sand, and logjams. Floods have kept the gravel bars open. Some banks have young alders where floodwaters reworked the channel, while in other spots large Douglas-firs grow to the river's edge, evidence that bank has been stable for a long time.

This morning I could see clearly the effects of the missing gravel and logs in the lower river. But in the dynamic upper river, it's harder to see what's gone. Biologists are only starting to realize how the loss of salmon, a keystone species, affects the entire ecosystem. The adult salmon returned only to spawn and die, and did not eat once they entered freshwater. But their carcasses were a major food source. Large predators like bald eagles and black bears dominated the feast on dying salmon, but many others joined. Raccoons, otters, skunks, mink, even Douglas squir-rels, deer mice, and shrews crept up to the gravel bars and fed on salmon. Among birds, not only the bald eagles and ravens but also gray jays and Steller's jays scavenged the decaying fish. Even winter wrens got beakfuls of salmon flesh. It's impossible to prove, but the large salmon runs prob-ably sustained more wildlife than now exists in the upper Elwha.

Scientists suspected for years that returning salmon contributed sig-nificant amounts of nutrients to Pacific Northwest watersheds, where heavy rains can leach the fertility out of soils and landslides strip soil from mountainsides. In the early 1990s, in a study done in the Snoqualmie River watershed east of Seattle, biologists traced distinctive isotopes of nitrogen and carbon that are found in the ocean and also in returning salmon. By looking for these stable isotopes in other life forms in the freshwater streams, the researchers were able to determine how much the dying salmon actually contributed nutritionally to the ecosystem.

The scientists found that marine-derived nitrogen made up from 18 to 30 percent of the nitrogen in the tissues of stream biota. The lower percentages were detected in some types of insect nymphs, and the high-est percentage was measured in juvenile coho salmon. The researchers also found that the young coho had a marked growth spurt after spawn-ing salmon arrived in the fall, possibly a result of the sudden flush of nutrients into the stream.

Adult salmon enrich the streams with their bodies, feeding a food chain of bacteria, fungi, aquatic insect larvae, and other tiny scavengers that in turn are food for young salmon. The salmon are a gift not just to humans fishing, but to the land and the rivers. Over time, the mountains slowly crumble into the rivers and wash to the sea, the rivers carry logs down-stream, and the salmon bring the nutrients from the ocean back to the mountains.

The absence of salmon has meant a significant loss of incoming nu-trients in the upper Elwha watershed for over eighty years now. Presum-ably, this loss translates to reduced numbers of animals in and near the river, from insects to bears, and a progressively declining ecosystem that will eventually stabilize at some lower level of productivity. But there are no biological inventories of these streams from before the dams, and so there is no way to know how much life has been diminished by the ab-sence of salmon.

Fisheries consultant Jim Lichatowich told me, "We're just beginning to figure out what happens when salmon aren't there. I think it is going to have a big effect. It will make recovery take longer. We need not just eggs in the gravel again, but nutrients supplied to the ecosystem again."

The Elwha is a classic case study of what dams do to rivers. It may also be our case study for what happens when we take dams out of rivers. In 1992, Congress passed a law authorizing the full restoration of the Elwha River ecosystem, including buying and removing the dams. The National Park Service has prepared a plan for tearing down the dams and restoring the salmon. If Congress funds the plan, the Elwha could be where we learn important lessons about how rivers heal after the dams are taken out.

THE ENVIRONMENTAL SOLUTION

Dams were the environmental solution of the early twentieth century. In the late 1800s, cities adopted electricity—produced by smoky coal-driven power plants located nearby—as their main source of power. Spokane had the first hydroelectric dam in the Pacific Northwest, built on the Spokane River in 1885. The first long-distance transmission of electricity in the world took place in Oregon in 1889, when a direct-current line was strung from Willamette Falls in Oregon City to Portland to power the streetlights. The invention of alternating current made it possible to transmit electric power over greater distances, and engineering advances made it feasible for the first time to dam rivers as large as the Columbia. Together, these early-twentieth-century discoveries opened the way for clean, renewable hydroelectric power produced at dams many miles away to replace electricity from air-polluting coal plants.

At the same time, the rivers that flowed through the Northwest's growing cities were becoming badly polluted. Every city along the Willamette dumped sewage directly into the river without any treatment. After development of the kraft, or sulfate, process in 1909 allowed formerly worthless wood to be turned into pulp for paper, the paper and pulp industry expanded rapidly. The pulp mills created large amounts of wastes, which they poured directly into rivers and estuaries, such as the Willamette and Puget Sound. Other industries also discharged their wastes into rivers.

The Willamette was one of the most heavily polluted rivers in the region. During the winter, high water flows diluted the wastes and flushed them down into the larger Columbia River, but during the summer, the Willamette was too low to thin the wastes significantly. On warm days, the stench was unbearable. By the early 1920s, the lower Willamette in Portland was almost completely devoid of dissolved oxygen in the summer. The river was unlivable for fish, and people were disgusted too.

Dams were proposed to solve the pollution problem. A network of dams across the Willamette's main forks and tributaries would control floods in the winter, hold back snowmelt runoff in the spring, and release water in the summer to raise water flows during the critical months of July, August, and September. Boosters of the dam project saw many benefits—the cities of the Willamette Valley would get both winter flood control and mitigation of summer pollution. Since little was known about river ecology, people believed that the year-round stability of river flows would benefit fish and rivers as well.

Through the 1920s and 1930s, many committees formed, and surveys were done, but no constructive action occurred. Water quality continued to worsen in the Willamette. In 1938, a statewide "Clean Rivers" ballot initiative passed by a margin of 3 to 1 and created a State Sanitary Authority, the precursor of Oregon's current Department of Environmental Quality. The new agency began its program in 1939, but the World War II years intervened, and it was many years before significant improvements were made in Willamette River water quality.

Demands for electricity, flood control, irrigation water, and waste dilution propelled the construction of large dams throughout the region. The National Reclamation Act of 1902 authorized the use of federal money for dam and irrigation projects and became an important mechanism for funding large dams. Another federal agency, the Army Corps of Engineers, also became a major dam-builder in the Pacific Northwest. World War I spurred the development of a regional transmission grid. Later, the Great Depression of the 1930s provided the impetus for large public works programs, which meant even more dams.

The dams in the Columbia River basin form the biggest hydropower system in the world. There are fourteen big dams on the Columbia mainstem and seven more on the Snake. Tributary rivers in the basin have hundreds of additional dams. Almost every tributary river in the American part of the basin has at least one dam, and many have several dams. The McKenzie watershed, which comprises only 0.5 percent of the Columbia River basin, has six dams. Even in a dry year, the dams of the Columbia River basin produce enough electricity for twelve cities the size of Seattle.

The Columbia River basin is crammed so full of dams that in all the long, twisting course of the Columbia in the United States, there is only one free-flowing stretch of river left above tidewater—the fifty-one-mile-long Hanford Reach in central Washington. Below Bonneville Dam, the river is affected by the tides, and above Bonneville, everything but the Hanford Reach is reservoirs. The Columbia Cascades, Celilo Falls,

Portland mayor Joe Carson and students campaigned for Oregon's Clean Rivers initiative in 1938, which passed by a 3 to 1 majority. (photo courtesy Oregon Historical Society, CN 001253)

The Dalles—all the famous falls and rapids of the Columbia—are drowned under the calm waters of reservoirs. The tail end of one reservoir backs up to the tailrace of the dam upriver from it. Only the Hanford Reach still has rapids, gravel bars, sloughs, and islands—the shape of a wild river—and it is loaded with species of fish, animals, and plants that have become rare or disappeared from the rest of the Columbia.

Rivers outside the Columbia basin were checked with dams too. The Klamath, Rogue, Umpqua, Snoqualmie, Skagit, and other major rivers were blocked, often with four, five, or more dams across their headwaters and main tributaries.

Only in the 1970s did the increasing expense of dam construction and strengthening environmental concerns slow and finally stop the building of major new dams in the Pacific Northwest. The Canadians completed Mica Dam on the upper Columbia in 1973. The Lower Granite Dam on the Snake River and Libby Dam on the Kootenai River in Montana went into operation in 1975, the last two large dams completed in the region. Other dam proposals were still on the books in various engineers' offices, but no one thought seriously that any more large dams would be built in the Pacific Northwest.

The dams provided all the benefits that their promoters promised. They fostered regional economic growth by producing a lot of cheap power. Several companies located energy-intensive aluminum smelters along the Columbia River to use the abundant, inexpensive power. The aluminum from their plants went into everything from soft drink cans to Boeing jets. Hydroelectricity helped produce french fries in Idaho, computer chips in Oregon, Microsoft software in Washington, and lumber, plywood, and paper throughout the three states. When the last dams were finished, three-fourths of the power in the Pacific Northwest was from hydroelectricity, and electricity rates were the cheapest in the nation. Water from reservoirs irrigated millions of acres in Idaho, Washington, and Oregon.

The dams also prevented floods. In just one example, the Willamette and Columbia River dams shaved the peak off the flood of February 1996. The Army Corps of Engineers manipulated water releases from more than sixty dams in the Willamette and Columbia River systems in order to reduce flooding in the Willamette Valley. Men and women in centralized control rooms managed river levels on hundreds of miles of rivers through complex negotiations and powerful computer systems.

When the heavy rain started, the Corps began holding water back in its eleven dams on the upper Willamette River and its tributaries. Cutting back water flow on the Columbia required international cooperation and a carefully orchestrated sequence. BC Hydro in British Columbia agreed to curb water releases from its Keenleyside Dam to lower the reservoir behind Grand Coulee Dam. In turn, Grand Coulee water releases were reduced from 160,000 cubic feet per second to 50,000 cubic feet per second. This cutback caused problems for Bonneville Power Administration (BPA), the federal agency that markets the power from most Columbia River dams. Despite the huge amounts of water pouring into the Columbia, BPA had to buy more-expensive electricity from elsewhere as it held back water releases. Next, three public utility districts agreed to check releases at mid-Columbia dams like Rocky Reach and Priest Rapids, even though the move forced them also to buy expensive electricity on the spot market. Finally the Corps of Engineers reduced water flow at their four big dams on the lower Columbia, and the level of the Columbia River actually dropped slightly downriver.

The cutbacks at the Willamette dams shaved the peak off the flood coming down the Willamette, and the maneuvers on the Columbia gave the Willamette more room to flow into the Columbia instead of backing up at the confluence and spreading out over Portland. After the flood, the engineers calculated that without the dams, the Willamette would have been 9 feet higher than it was in Eugene, 7 feet higher in Salem, and 6 to 8 feet higher in Portland. As it turned out, the Willamette stopped rising an inch or two below the top of the seawall through downtown Portland, at a level of 28.6 feet.

DISRUPTION

The dams were also cataclysmic events for the rivers. Just as on the Elwha, the effects cascaded upstream and downstream. On rivers plugged repeatedly by dams, such as the Columbia and the Snake, the effects extended for hundreds of miles.

Grand Coulee is the flagship of Pacific Northwest dams. It generates roughly three times as much electricity as the region's second biggest power producer, the John Day Dam. Grand Coulee helped win World War II: coming on-line in 1941, it powered both the factories that made the aluminum for American aircraft and Hanford Nuclear Reservation, a critical facility in the country's drive to create nuclear bombs. Grand Coulee is also the dam that did the greatest damage to Columbia River basin salmon runs.

Salmon used to migrate to the Columbia headwaters and upper Columbia tributaries, over a thousand miles from the ocean. The upper Columbia chinook could be a hundred pounds or more, big fish that could travel over a thousand miles upstream against a powerful current without feeding. Millions of salmon climbed the fish ladders up Bonneville and past Rock Island, the two dams on the lower river when Grand Coulee was completed. But a fish ladder for the huge Grand Coulee Dam would have been many miles long, and the dam was built without any attempt to provide fish passage. In one magnificent sweep of concrete, Grand Coulee blocked hundreds of miles of prime salmon habitat.

Grand Coulee was not the only dam built without fish passage. In 1916, the aptly named Iron Gate Dam was closed across the Klamath River a few miles south of the Oregon border, cutting off salmon access to southern Oregon's upper Klamath Basin. Hells Canyon Dam on the Snake River kept salmon from all of the upper Snake River and its tributaries. Dworshak Dam intercepted the Clearwater River in Idaho, resulting in the extinction of the steelhead and chinook runs that used to head up that river. Dexter and Lookout Point blocked the Willamette River, Cougar Dam blocked the McKenzie, Pelton Dam blocked the Deschutes. Chief Joseph Dam was built downstream from Grand Coulee and checked another fifty miles of the Columbia, not much compared with Grand Coulee, but another piece of river closed off. When all the construction dust had settled, one-third of the salmon and steelhead habitat in the Columbia River basin, and an unknown amount of salmon habitat outside the basin, were blocked by impassable dams—thousands of miles, much of it relatively pristine headwater reaches. Across the Pacific Northwest, dozens of salmon stocks were extirpated simply because of dams without fish passage.

For the dams designed to be passable, fish ladders were reasonably successful for upstream passage. But engineers failed to consider downstream passage for the salmon smolts migrating to the ocean. Many of the juvenile fish passed through the turbines, where they were chopped up by the blades, injured or stunned by the tremendous force of the water, or trapped in the backroll wave below the dam. Those that escaped the turbines dropped over spillways. If they weren't killed in the fall, they often died below the dams in water supersaturated with nitrogen gas, which formed small bubbles in their blood vessels and interfered with normal blood flow. The Northwest Power Planning Council has estimated that 10 to 30 percent of migrating salmon smolts die at each dam on the Columbia and Snake Rivers. Smolts coming from Idaho rivers have to get past eight dams. The completion of the final four dams on the Snake River in the late 1960s and early 1970s seemed to be the critical point at which smolt mortality became so high that runs already in decline crashed to extremely low numbers.

The reservoirs are an additional hazard for the smolts. Before the rivers were converted into a series of slackwater reservoirs, the young salmon took about three weeks to get from the Salmon River in Idaho to the Columbia below Bonneville, carried down by the swift current of the spring runoff. It now takes smolts seven to eight weeks to make the same trip. They use much of their small energy reserves to swim the length of the reservoirs and are exposed to predatory fish in the reservoirs for a longer period of time.

The agencies that operate the dams and manage the fish have tried many expensive solutions. They have captured smolts at the upper end of the reservoirs and barged them downriver, releasing them below Bonneville. They have developed screens for turbines and elaborate bypasses to keep fish away from the turbines, and have equipped spillways with "flip lips" to minimize injuries and reduce nitrogen gas. On an experimental basis, they have tried drawing down some of the reservoirs so the Snake and Columbia flow more like natural rivers. All the solutions cost millions of dollars, and all are trying to do what the rivers used to do for free and what the salmon smolts used to do on their own.

The hatcheries—more than eighty in the Columbia River basin alone—produced salmon fry that hadn't gone through natural genetic selection and that sometimes carried hatchery-spread diseases. Often stocks were transplanted from their native watershed to a hatchery in a different watershed, and the fry did not have the local adaptations of the watershed's native stocks. Millions of these salmon fry were released into rivers that often didn't have enough food for salmon any more. Overfishing continued in the lower Columbia and in the ocean.

The dam builders believed in techno-fixes. They approached fish passage as an engineering problem and fish abundance as a production problem. They believed they could produce more salmon the same way they could produce more motors at a factory. They did not understand that the dams and reservoirs created enormous ecological disruptions that reverberated the entire length of the rivers.

Salmon got the most attention, but the dams devastated dozens of species, from freshwater fish, to amphibians, to native snails and clams. Dams blocked normal upstream and downstream migrations for freshwater fish, amphibians, and insects with aquatic larvae. Stoneflies, mayflies, caddisflies, and other insects with aquatic larvae normally travel only short distances as adults, usually upstream, before laying eggs in or near the water. Adults often live only a few hours or a few days. They are too weak and their lives too short to migrate the entire distance of a miles-long reservoir to the free-flowing water they need. Thus, big dams and long reservoirs effectively cut them off from upper river reaches.

Dams broke the continuous ranges of many freshwater fish species into isolated populations and often cut them off from their spawning areas.

Dams and Salmon Habitat in the Columbia River Basin

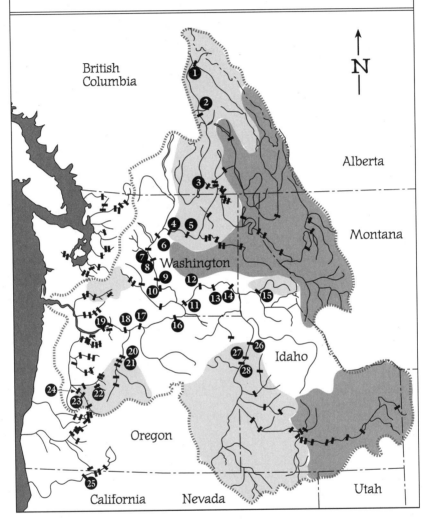

Hundreds of dams have been built on Pacific Northwest rivers. This map shows just the larger dams in the region. In the Columbia River basin, dams built without fish passage block one-third of the habitat originally available to salmon and steelhead. Some dams outside the basin also block salmon habitat. The blocked habitat outside the Columbia River basin is not shown.

Dams and Salmon Habitat in the Columbia River Basin

Map Legend

ıııııı Watershed boundary

▢ Salmon habitat blocked by dams

▢ Salmon habitat blocked by natural barriers

Dam Location Legend

❶ Mica	⓫ Ice Harbor	㉑ Pelton
❷ Revelstoke	⓬ Lower Monument	㉒ Cougar
❸ Keenleyside	⓭ Little Goose	㉓ Lookout Point
❹ Chief Joseph	⓮ Lower Granite	㉔ Dexter
❺ Grand Coulee	⓯ Dworshak	㉕ Iron Gate
❻ Wells	⓰ McNary	㉖ Hells Canyon
❼ Rocky Reach	⓱ John Day	㉗ Oxbow
❽ Rock Island	⓲ The Dalles	㉘ Brownlee
❾ Wanapum	⓳ Bonneville	
❿ Priest Rapids	⓴ Pelton Reregulating	

Source: Based on maps from *Daily/Hourly Hydrosystem Operation: How the Columbia River System Responds to Short-Term Needs,* by Bonneville Power Administration et al., 1994, and *Columbia River Basin Fish and Wildlife Program—Strategy for Salmon, Volume I,* by Northwest Power Planning Council, 1992.

White sturgeon, which can grow to over twelve feet long and to more than a thousand pounds, live in the Northwest's larger rivers—such as the Columbia, the Snake, and the Kootenai—the same rivers that are so heavily dammed. These giant fish need flowing water to spawn—they cannot reproduce successfully in slackwater reservoirs. Snake River white sturgeon used to inhabit the river from its mouth to Shoshone Falls. Now, the only free-flowing section of the Snake in the three-hundred-mile stretch between its mouth and the top of Brownlee Reservoir is the Hells Canyon Reach, and there the highest density of Snake River white sturgeon is found. The prognosis is uncertain for the long-term survival of the other populations of Snake River white sturgeon.

The Kootenai River white sturgeon have been isolated naturally between Kootenai Falls and Bonnington Falls since the end of the Ice Age. Apparently the population has not had any successful reproduction since Libby Dam went into operation upriver in 1975. Biologists believe the spawning failures are due to reduced springtime river flows, the result of Libby Dam holding back the spring snowmelt flood. Since white sturgeon are extremely long-lived, the Kootenai population still survives, but they need to have successful spawning years soon or the aging population will die out. If a new proposal is adopted to release more water from the dam during the spring spawning season, the sturgeon may succeed in reproducing. However, biologists do not know yet if the water release alone will help the fish.

Isolated fish populations are vulnerable to genetic bottlenecks and local extinctions. If disease or a large natural disturbance wipes out an isolated population, the fish cannot recolonize the area from refugia. Over time, as small populations disappear and are not replenished, the species begins to disappear from more and more of its range.

Bull trout are aggressive predators that live only in extremely cold, very clean water. The species always had a limited range in western Oregon, living in only a few of its coldest rivers. Now, the McKenzie River has the only surviving bull trout population in Oregon west of the Cascades crest. Cougar Dam on the South Fork and Trail Bridge Dam on the mainstem divided the McKenzie bull trout into three small, isolated populations: one above each dam and a third in the McKenzie mainstem. When the McKenzie Highway was extended along the upper McKenzie in the 1960s, poorly designed culverts blocked the trout's access to several spawning streams, leaving the largest population with only two springbrooks where they could reproduce. The survival of the two isolated populations, South Fork and Trail Bridge, is now uncertain. They have had some years with no spawning success and only limited success in other years. The survival of bull trout in western Oregon now depends on the mainstem McKenzie population.

The reservoirs behind the dams also disrupted river ecosystems. These artificial lakes created new ecosystems, more like warm, slow, muddy Midwestern rivers than cold, clear, fast-flowing Pacific Northwest rivers.

Midwestern fish species were introduced and flourished in the changed habitats: walleye, crappies, catfish, northern pike, bass, bluegills, and yellow perch, among other species. These new species created additional problems for native fish.

Forest Service scientist Gordon Reeves explained some of the problems to me: "For example, walleye is a schooling predator that hunts at night. Salmon smolts migrate at night, because native predators did not hunt at night. Also, the exotic predatory fish have larger mouths."

The river water warms up as it passes slowly through the strings of reservoirs, and the warmer water affects fish, too. "The altered temperatures may not be lethal in themselves," Gordon said, "but cause shifts in the fish community. Temperatures just a few degrees higher favor shiners instead of salmonids, and make it difficult for salmon to compete." The warmer water also speeds up the salmon smolts' metabolism, and they have trouble eating enough to replenish the additional calories they are burning.

Reservoirs are flood and nutrient sinks. They absorb floods, wood, sediment—everything coming downriver—like a great still pond. The water still gets downstream, eventually, but the river is robbed of its texture, of the chunkiness in the current that renews the river channel.

Since the lower reaches of rivers are usually the most degraded, the best remaining refugia in most watersheds are the upper ends of the basins. But often these refugia are blocked by dams. So, finally, the dams block fish and other survivors in the lower reaches from reaching the upstream refugia, and at the same time the dams contribute to the degradation of the lower rivers.

"It's not just the salmon that are in trouble," said Gordon Reeves, "but all native fish."

THE HYDROGRAPH

One of the Bonneville Power Administration documents in my library has a hydrograph of the Columbia River from 1878 to 1991, measured at The Dalles. Like a cardiogram for a river, the thin line of the hydrograph shows the rises and falls in the river flow. For the first hundred years, one large pulse occurred every year sometime between May and July, when the spring snowmelt in the mountains caused the Columbia's annual spring flood. Other smaller rises and dips were only wobbles in the main pattern. I can trace the river's history year by year through the peaks and troughs of the line.

Native Americans fished at Celilo Falls on the Columbia River until it was drowned behind The Dalles Dam in 1956. (photo courtesy Oregon Historical Society, OrHi 92427, Boychuck photo)

PULSE. The salmon smolts were flushed from their mountain streams by a rising river and carried hundreds of miles to the ocean. *PULSE.* The river reopened old side channels and rushed through them. *PULSE.* The famous Columbia River spring chinook runs started to decline, and the harvest of sockeye, chum, coho, and steelhead increased. *PULSE.* The river floated trees dropped by winter storms and carried them toward the ocean. *PULSE.* All Columbia River salmon runs were declining. *PULSE.* The riverbed cobbles were scrubbed clean of silt by the spring flood. Snails like the shortface lanx, nerite rams-horn, and Columbia pebblesnail were common in the river. *PULSE.* The first big dams were built across the river, but were not enough to substantially reduce the spring flood. *PULSE*. The tidal swamps and low-lying islands of the lower Columbia estuary were sculpted and renewed by the spring flood. *PULSE*. In 1948, a twenty-day flood on the Columbia destroyed the city of Vanport, Oregon, an area now part of Portland, and killed thirty-two people. More flood control dams were planned. *PULSE*. Native Americans fished their last season at Celilo Falls in 1956. As more dams came on-line, the strength of the yearly flood pulse lessened. The peak on the hydrograph was lower. *Pulse*. Through the 1960s, the pulse got weaker every year. *Pulse*. By 1969, the yearly flood pulse was only a faint beat. And then, from 1975 on, nothing. A flat line.

Chapter 6

The Simplified Landscape

O ne way to discover the history of Pacific Northwest watersheds is
through books, journals, and archives. But a landscape's past reveals itself in the land and rivers today. When we learn how to interpret
the evidence, then the frequency of meanders in a watercourse, the presence or absence of cottonwoods on the banks, the abundance of deep
pools, the residence of mayfly nymphs and native trout tell us the history of a river and its basin.

THE JOHN DAY RIVER
The John Day River flows through eastern Oregon and into the Columbia roughly thirty miles east of The Dalles. It doesn't pass through the
country's deepest gorge like the Snake River, which runs through Hells
Canyon to the east; or through the spectacular Wallowa Mountains, like
the Grande Ronde and Imnaha. It is less dramatic and less famous than
these other rivers and so is lightly visited by tourists. It was also over-
looked during the century-long engineering boom to improve rivers and
fisheries. The John Day was never dammed, and no hatchery salmon were
ever introduced in the basin. Because it was bypassed, the John Day River
is a stronghold for wild salmon and steelhead in the interior Columbia
Basin. Runs of wild spring chinook, fall chinook, and steelhead still return to its spawning gravels.

   The John Day's four main forks curl out of the Blue Mountain forests and eventually merge to wind through high desert country, a dry
landscape of short grasses, sagebrush, and juniper. The river cuts

through fossil beds in several places that have scientific significance but are little known to the general public.

In many ways, the history of the John Day Basin, Oregon's fourth largest watershed, is representative of most eastside rivers. In the 1820s, Peter Skene Ogden, a fur trader, found that beavers were abundant along the river and that the banks had gallery forests of cottonwoods, aspens, poplars, and willows. The water was deep enough in summer that Ogden was unable to ford his horses across it near Prairie City. Although the John Day flowed through a dry landscape, its riparian forests stored moisture and turned the watercourse into a long green corridor through the high desert.

After the fur trapping era, white settlement in the John Day Basin started with a gold rush in 1862 along the upper mainstem near Canyon City and along the Middle and North Forks. The early placer mining was later replaced by dredge mining, which continued on the North Fork until 1950. Dredge mining chewed up the floodplain and riverbed and everything on it—willows, creek dogwoods, stonefly nymphs clinging to rocks—then spit it all back out into rock piles. The mined reaches were left with fifteen-foot-high heaps of stone covering their floodplains. Confined to a single, narrow channel, the river was unable to spread out during floods and instead dug down deeper into its channel, further isolating itself from the surrounding lands. The former floodplain never got the chance to absorb spring runoff and store the water. As a result, the snowmelt ran off quickly in spring, and the river level dropped sharply in summer.

As soon as the initial gold rush spurred settlement, other land uses began. Cattle grazing started in the 1860s, at first lower in the watershed, especially near the towns of Clarno and Shaniko. Sheep grazing began in the 1880s. By the 1900s, when the railroad came through, the little settlement of Shaniko was an enormous shipping center for wool. Flocks were so large that the clumps of sheep on the hillsides looked like drifts of snow. Eastern Oregon's native bunchgrasses were not adapted to this kind of grazing pressure and were unable to recover. Exotic species like cheatgrass became established and soon dominated the range.

Logging entered the Blue Mountains in 1862. The Blue Mountain Forest Reserve, which was later divided into three national forests, was established in 1906. By the 1920s, logging and lumber mills had become major industries in the basin. Timber harvest levels increased on the three national forests until about 1950, then remained at a steady level through

The riverbanks are bare where cattle have unrestricted access to this segment of the Middle Fork of the John Day River. (Gene Skrine)

the mid-1990s. Irrigation farming also got under way early in the John Day River valley. Although parts of the Blue Mountains were protected as wilderness areas and the population never got very large in the John Day Basin, the river and its watershed were dramatically changed by the many land uses.

On the day in late August that my husband, Gene, and I drive into the John Day Valley, sprinkler systems are spraying water on fields of alfalfa, pumpkins, and gourds. We see a few scattered clumps of cotton-woods and willows along the river. The mainstem is shallow and silty through the town of John Day. As we travel into the Blue Mountains to head down the Middle Fork, we watch smoke plumes in the Strawberry Mountain Wilderness south of us and bigger plumes over the ridge to the northeast: forest fires sparked by a dry lightning storm a few days earlier.

The Middle Fork of the John Day is just a small stream running through pasture along its upper reaches. The cattle roaming in the valley have free access to the river. No shrubs or trees grow along the riparian edge, just short grass, with the bank trampled to bare dirt in spots where the cattle have walked down into the water. A great blue heron stands at the side of a riffle. Ponderosa and lodgepole pines grow on the valley's gently sloping sides.

Below Deerhorn Camp, we see smoke in the east again. The fire has three main heads, which are merging into one smoke column that billows up thousands of feet like a thunderhead, then spreads into a long gray smear across the sky. Although the blaze is on the far side of the ridge, we can see dark gray and orange colors in the smoke right above the ridge top, evidence of the tremendous heat boiling up from the burning forest. I watch a retardant plane make a drop, and a helicopter wheels above the ridge for a few seconds, then descends back into the fire area again.

The river flows through national forest land, then another private ranch. This stretch has lusher grass that is still green in late summer, and some alders, hawthorn, and pines along the river. I see mussel shells in one pool. Four osprey wheel and cry above their nest, the fledglings already almost as big as their parents.

The Nature Conservancy has a 1,222-acre preserve here, a former ranch now being managed for the benefit of the river and wild salmon. The preserve manager, Ramon Lara, tells me that the river used to meander more through this valley. It looped through side channels in places and was slower, deeper, and cooler. Now the straightened watercourse is faster, shallower, and warmer. With volunteer work parties and a small staff, Ramon is working to restore the old river form, riparian habitats, and natural water flows. In 1997, he plans to reopen a onetime meander closed off by a previous landowner.

The preserve has been closed to cattle grazing since 1990, when The Nature Conservancy bought the land. Gene and I wander along the river through the protected area. Cottonwoods, alders, water birches, creek dogwoods, hawthorns, and snowberries grow on the banks, shading much of the water. I notice old beaver chew marks on a fallen cottonwood. The grass is mostly knee-high and reaches almost hip-high in a few areas. Sedges and bulrushes are thick and lush along the channel edges. Ponderosa pines dominate the forest on the hillsides. Patches of teasel and thistles grow in the meadows away from the riparian zone—invasive, nonnative weeds that crowd out the native grasses and flowers.

Downriver from the preserve, separated by a fence, is another private ranch. Its pasture has grass only two to three inches tall. The river is open to the cattle, and its banks are bare, without a single shrub along this reach. We drive downriver, then turn east and start to follow the North Fork upriver.

Gene and I camp at the junction of Desolation Creek and the North Fork. A sign points up the road to the Bull Complex fire camp, and fire camp traffic rumbles by all night—food delivery trucks, water trucks, gas truck, crew buses, pickup trucks. The next day, we explore the North Fork.

The North Fork of the John Day flows out of wilderness on national forest land. It's opening day of archery season, and hunting parties are camped at most flat spots along the river, on the way to the wilderness trailheads. The North Fork has a lot more water than the Middle Fork or the mainstem. We drive up the dirt lane until we reach a road closure, and from there we walk upriver. Smoky haze dims the sun.

A doodlebug gold dredge on pontoons worked its way up the North Fork from 1939 to 1950. We hike past hundreds of dredge piles, running up first one side of the river, then the middle, then the other side. Floods have partially broken down the rock heaps on the upstream edge of each string of piles and jammed driftwood logs against them, but most of the stacks are intact, almost fifty years after the end of mining. Their bases are made of granite boulders not easily moved by even a strong current. Elderberries, hawthorns, and creek dogwoods grow along the edges of the mounds, but the rock heaps themselves are barren. Ponderosa pines cover the hillsides.

Gene puts his hand on my arm and points. In a deep pool alongside a chain of dredge piles, I see about twenty chinook. They are waiting for fall. When the water temperature cools and the river flow increases, they will spawn. The three-foot salmon are long, dark shapes in the water. They hold facing upstream, almost in parallel rows, moving just enough to stay in place. Occasionally one swims to a new spot and then holds its new position. These fish are spring chinook and have already been here one or two months. Several are mottled with streaks of white fungus. They have about one more month to wait. By the time they mate, their bodies will be starting to rot. The salmon will have just enough energy left to spawn before they die and give their bodies back to the river.

A large beaver lodge sits on the edge of another pool upstream. Several twelve-inch trout look small when they swim past the half dozen salmon in the deep water. The trout have nothing to fear; these salmon haven't eaten since they left the ocean, and they won't eat again.

Eventually I find a pool without any salmon, and I turn over small stones to see what's living here. I see snails, mayfly nymphs, and caddisfly larvae. A dry rock at the channel's edge has several molted husks clinging to it, the cast-off skins of stonefly nymphs that emerged from the river to take to the air as winged adults.

We don't get past the dredge piles until we get to the wilderness boundary. As I walk up Big Creek Trail, the canyon gets narrower and moister. The forest has a few ponderosa pines, but here it is mixed with Douglas-firs, true firs, mountain ash, and alders. Bracken ferns, clover, and Solomon's seal grow beneath the trees.

The forest on the north slope looks as if it burned about ten or fifteen years ago, judging by the age of young trees among the blackened snags. Some of the fire-killed pines have already fallen; others will fall into the river in a few years, renewing the supply of driftwood. Here in the wilderness—past the Columbia River dams, the grazing, irrigation, logging,

Gold dredges chewed up riverbeds, damaging and simplifying complex river systems and leaving miles of dredge piles behind. (photo courtesy Oregon Historical Society, OrHi 39565)

and dredge piles—the old patterns of disturbance and renewal—fire, flood, and resilience—continue. The air has been smoky all day long, but it gets worse as the forest fires west and north of us make their biggest runs in the heat of the afternoon. I can see the towering column of smoke from one fire behind a distant ridge.

Gene and I are observing a river that is far from pristine. Over the last 150 years, land uses have damaged the river, severely in some places. The mining, grazing, irrigation, and logging weakened the ecosystem, leading it toward collapse. But wild salmon still return to it, and stoneflies thrive. A ragged patchwork of refugia, including the wilderness and healthier spots outside it, holds the threads of the damaged system together. In fact, the John Day River is in better shape than many others. Several restoration projects are under way in the watershed, including a Forest Service operation to rebuild the floodplain on the North Fork and The Nature Conservancy work on the Middle Fork. These two undertakings, which are described in Chapter 9, are examples of the best restoration approaches we know today.

WATERSHEDS AND LAND USES

Simplify, simplify. It's good advice for people, but a bad idea for rivers. Our land use practices have simplified river ecosystems throughout the Pacific Northwest.

In Oregon and Washington east of the Cascades, the extensive grasslands were overgrazed by sheep and cattle as early as the late 1800s. Livestock tended to clump along streams on hot, dry summer days, where they trampled riparian shrubs and grasses. Stream banks were eroded and streambeds disrupted, not by a yearly flood, but by frequent pounding from hooves.

The grazing declined after World War I. Since then, most rangelands in Oregon and Washington have not supported the numbers of livestock they once had. Some lightly populated eastern Washington watersheds partially recovered after grazing pressure dropped, but in other watersheds, irrigation farming and logging were already increasing.

Truly large-scale irrigation projects did not begin until 1902, when the Reclamation Act made federal funding available. By the 1980s, somewhere between 6 and 8 million acres were irrigated in the states of Idaho, Oregon, and Washington. The major irrigated areas were the Snake River plain, the Yakima Basin, the Wenatchee Basin, the Okanogan Valley, the Columbia Basin from Moses Lake to Pasco, the Umatilla Basin, and the Klamath Lakes Basin. Some irrigation went on in areas west of the

Irrigation can disrupt rivers in many ways. This pool for an irrigation pump was dug into a gravel bar (Umatilla River). (Gene Skrine)

Cascades, such as Oregon's Willamette Valley and the Dungeness River on the Olympic Peninsula. The eastside irrigated areas were only islands of green in the dry landscape of the interior, but their impacts on streams were significant.

Irrigation in the Columbia River basin used only about 6 percent of the basin's total stream flow. The wheat, corn, potatoes, peas, apples, grapes, and other crops produced seemed well worth the price of the water withdrawal, much of which eventually ran back into the rivers as irrigation return flow. But in rivers like the Yakima and Umatilla, summer water withdrawals left some stretches of riverbed almost dry. The water left dribbling in the channels got lethally warm or was polluted with agricultural runoff. Salmon smolts were blocked from migrating downstream, and returning adult fish could not reach their spawning areas.

Western water rights laws were designed to protect "beneficial uses" of water, which included every use of water as a commodity—for irrigation, drinking, industry, and livestock—but did not require any water to be left in the rivers. According to the law, fish were last in line for water rights. By the late 1980s, Pacific Northwest states began to establish minimum instream flows on some rivers in order to protect fish and river ecosystems. Unfortunately, the minimum flows were new water rights held by state agencies and were junior to other water rights. Senior water rights would be satisfied first. In some rivers, fish might be waiting for years.

Irrigation withdrawals diverted more than water from the rivers. In the early 1900s, one federal fish biologist estimated that 4.5 million juvenile salmon were lost in the Yakima Basin every time the fields were watered, which was about every ten days. Serious screening of water diversions started in the 1930s, but it took years to develop effective screens. Some irrigators never complied with regulations, or failed to maintain the devices. As late as the 1990s, the Columbia Basin Salmon Enforcement Team, an interagency team, was still finding cases in which young salmon were pumped out onto fields along with river water.

Rivers were channelized and wetlands drained throughout the Pacific Northwest, both east and west of the Cascades. The Willamette, the lower Columbia, and the rivers of lower Puget Sound had been channelized early. In other areas, such as southern Oregon's Klamath Basin, the changes came later.

Upper Klamath Lake is Oregon's largest freshwater lake. The Williamson River used to wander through a braided delta and a complex mosaic of marshes before it flowed into the lake's northeast corner. Dense thickets of willows and cottonwoods grew on the banks of the meandering channels. Millions of ducks and geese migrated to the marshes in the winter. Sandhill cranes mated, and bald eagles preyed on the ducks. Spring and fall chinook returned to the Williamson and Sprague Rivers. The Klamath Basin had eight species of fish unique to the basin, including the Lost River sucker and shortnose sucker, which were major food sources for the Klamath Indians. The rivers renewed the marshes through annual floods.

The federal government began building the Klamath reclamation project in 1905, damming the lake mouth to control the water level. The Williamson River was straightened and diked so it flowed through one channel directly into the lake. Levees were constructed to separate the marshes from the river, and the wetlands were drained and turned into irrigated fields. Only 10 percent of the original marshes remain around Upper Klamath Lake. Cattle graze on the former marshlands, and irrigated fields grow grains, sugar beets, and other crops.

Most of the remaining marshes are protected in wildlife refuges, and the Klamath Basin still attracts the largest concentration of wintering bald eagles outside Alaska. But the number of waterfowl supported in the basin has dropped by millions of birds. The salmon are gone, blocked by the

Iron Gate Dam. The Lost River sucker and shortnose sucker were both listed as endangered species in 1988. The few remaining fish spawn in the Williamson River, but deprived of the marshes they need for food and cover, most young fish die before they can return to the lake. Upper Klamath Lake now has large blooms of blue-green algae every summer, which create a foul-smelling scum and deplete the water of oxygen. Surface runoff from grazing and agriculture is suspected to be a main cause of the excessive growth. The Klamath Indians no longer harvest the suckers. Instead, each year the tribe captures one live fish. Tribal elders bless the fish in a ceremony and then place it back into the river.

Simplified rivers look recovered after a few years. In fact, biologists don't know how long it takes severely degraded waterways to recuperate because they have never seen one recover on its own. Channelized streams are almost completely severed from their watersheds. Riprapped banks and levees usually stop rivers from reinhabiting their old floodplains

Driftwood logs are the backbone of a healthy stream (McKenzie River side channel). (Gene Skrine)

and side channels. Richly textured channels with meanders, pools, riffles, and logjams are replaced by straight runs of riffling water. The riparian areas may be narrowed to thin lines of alders and cottonwoods that no longer have the ability to buffer a stream from events in the watershed, and that contribute little to the stream. Cobbled rivers once rich with young salmon, trout, sculpins, beavers, mergansers, osprey, and eagles are turned into simple canals with greatly diminished life.

FORESTS AND RIVERS

Of all the land use practices that affect rivers, forestry has gotten the most attention. Approximately 46 percent of Oregon, Washington, and Idaho is covered by forests. This figure includes all forests: federal forests, some of which are protected as wilderness or by other designations; privately owned commercial forest lands; state forests; tribal forests; and noncommercial forest lands. The total amount of forest in the region has dropped slightly since the early 1800s, mainly because some forest lands were converted to farms or cities.

The Pacific Northwest timber industry took off at the end of the nineteenth century. Loggers moved here as forests in the Great Lakes states were depleted and new railroads opened national markets for Northwest logs. From 1898 to 1914, Oregon and Idaho tripled their timber production. Washington was the country's leading timber state from 1905 to 1938, when Oregon passed it to hold top place for nearly fifty years.

Although the last 150 years of logging have not changed the total number of acres in forests very much, they have greatly altered the nature of the forests. The forests of the early 1800s were a mixture of old growth, recent burns, and forests of different ages recovering naturally from fires. In 1850, 40 percent of western Oregon forests were older than 200 years, and just over a third were burned areas beginning to recover. Today's forests have more acreage in young trees and less in old growth. They have roads, culverts, and bridges. Logging removed much of the biological legacy of fires—the standing dead trees and fallen trees that helped the forests and streams recover.

Source of map, opposite: This map was created by Sara Freedman in October, 1996 for the Natural Resources Conservation Service in Portland, Oregon. Floodplain areas were generated from Natural Resources Conservation Service STATSGO general soils maps where 10% or more of the soils are subject to rare, occasional, or frequent flooding. Rivers files are from Bonneville Power Administration at 1:250,000 base scale.

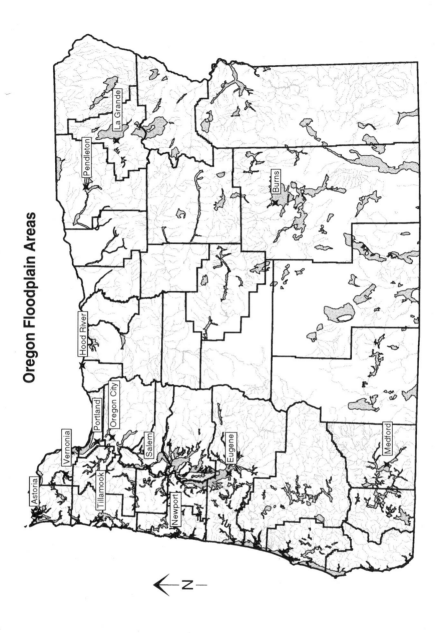

Oregon Floodplain Areas

La Grande
Pendleton
Burns
Hood River
Portland
Oregon City
Vernonia
Salem
Eugene
Medford
Astoria
Tillamook
Newport

←N–

Historically, Pacific Northwest rivers in lowland valleys had large floodplains. Despite a century of flood control projects, rivers still occasionally reclaim their historic floodplains.

Scientists began to study the effects of logging on streams in the 1950s. The forested river valleys had been logged already, so researchers focused their attention on headwater streams in the mountains where logging was still going on. Over the years, they started to tease out the complicated links between trees, roads, and streams.

The total amount of fish biomass in streams actually increased right after clear-cutting. More sunlight reached the water, the algae production multiplied, and algae blooms fueled a growth spurt up the entire food chain. But the burst of activity was short-lived. Then streams started to unravel.

The loss of streamside trees deprived small streams of their most important food source—leaves, needles, and twigs. The food web changed. After the initial growth spurt, fish abundance and diversity usually declined. As new areas were logged and more shade was lost, the water warmed up, and the higher temperatures made survival more difficult for trout and juvenile salmon.

Large fallen trees were the backbones of the small streams. Without them, the streams lost much of their structure and stability. Complex stream margins were reduced to simple edges. Streams were unable to store and digest leaves and needles. They also lost their ability to handle sediments and were smothered by gravel and dirt carried downstream by freshets. And after a mountainside was logged, there was a lot of incoming sediment.

A pulse of surface erosion entered streams for several years after a mountainside was first logged. As grasses and shrubs covered the ground, the topsoil stabilized quickly. But logging on steep slopes led to an increased risk of landslides for ten to thirty years afterward. The landslides moved huge masses of soil, with far more earth lost during slides than through the temporary sheet erosion.

Clear-cut logging and forest roads increased the rate of landslides and debris flows by two to forty times over the frequency in wilderness areas. Many variables affected the rate of landslides, including underlying geology, slope steepness, climate, road design, and logging practices.

Some landslides were natural in the steep mountains and wet climate of the Pacific Northwest, but logging changed the natural disturbances in three ways. It increased the frequency of slides. It also changed the texture of slides from chunky to silty, since the trees had been removed. Finally, logging simplified the streams, and they no longer had the capacity to absorb landslides. The slides often gouged streams to bedrock for long distances instead of being slowed by logjams.

Winter floods were relatively common in the Willamette Valley before the dams were built during the mid-1900s (Corvallis, south city limits). (photo courtesy Oregon Historical Society, OrHi 67901)

Foresters gradually responded to the new information. Oregon passed its Forest Practices Act in 1971 and has updated it several times since. Washington and Idaho also adopted forest practices laws. Over the years, the U.S. Forest Service and Bureau of Land Management modified their logging practices. Loggers were required to leave trees along stream banks, to change road-building techniques, to suspend logs with cables as they yarded logs to landings, and to keep equipment out of streams.

Despite improvements in forest practices, in the 1980s and 1990s evidence grew that the cumulative effects of a century of logging were much worse than anyone had realized. Each logged unit affected the streams below it for a considerable distance. As more and more patches were cut, the effects multiplied. Logging roads spread over the steep slopes like webbing that would some day be pulled tight, catching the mountains like a snared animal. All the forest practices acts required replanting, and the harvest units were filled with young conifers in a few years. But the finger-thin young trees needed at least fifty to a hundred years before they would be much help to streams.

The Simplified Landscape   119

The old U.S. Bureau of Fisheries (now the National Marine Fisheries Service) had surveyed five thousand miles of streams in the Columbia River basin between 1936 and 1942. Two Forest Service scientists, Jim Sedell and Fred Everest, realized that the old surveys gave them a chance to see how the streams had changed over fifty years. Crews resurveyed over three hundred miles of the streams in the late 1980s.

The survey crews found that habitat quality had stayed relatively constant in streams that flowed through wilderness areas. But streams that flowed through watersheds where logging had occurred had lost from 50 to 75 percent of their large pools over the last fifty years. In 1937, streams with little timber harvest had an average of more than fifteen large pools for every stream mile. In the late 1980s, after moderate logging in those watersheds, the same streams had less than seven large pools per mile. Streams lost deep pools because they had lost logjams and meanders, the structures that had created and maintained the pools. More fine sediments had entered streams after logging and filled the pools.

Sedell and Everest's study was unique because it had data from fifty years ago for comparison. Stream surveys were not common in the past. Generally, scientists have only a few years of records when they study the effects of logging on streams.

However, one finding has been consistent through all the studies on the effects of forest management on streams. Logging, road building, and other forest practices have simplified streams. They have lost deep pools, large wood, riparian forests, and complex habitats. Instead of having a variety of gravels, cobbles, and fine sediments on their beds, streams have been left with more homogeneous beds. They have lost much of their capacity to store and digest leaves, wood, and other organic matter, the stuff that fuels the food web. The changes have cascaded through the aquatic communities from insect larvae to larger fish. Some species have become scarce or disappeared. Life history patterns have been changed and sometimes lost. Altered food webs have lost links and entire strands, sometimes becoming more like ladders than webs.

THE H.J. ANDREWS FOREST AND THE FLOOD

If I load a handgun and leave it on top of my dresser, dust gathering on the shiny black steel, maybe nothing would ever happen. Years might go by peacefully without a shot being fired. But some day, perhaps in twenty years, someone might pick it up and pull the trigger. The result might be harmless, just a bullet in the ceiling, or it might be tragic. For rivers, logging is like loading the gun. Rainstorms pull the trigger.

The February flood of 1996 pulled triggers on loaded guns all over the region. Landslides devastated houses, roads, and land. People died. Dirt poured into rivers. The Federal Emergency Management Agency (FEMA) statistics would show eventually how devastating the flood was for people and their homes, farms, livestock, roads, and other developments. Another federal agency, the Forest Service, took the lead on investigating the event's effects on rivers and how much forest management practices contributed to the flood.

After the flood, while homeowners were tearing out ruined carpets and highway crews were repairing roads, the scientists of the H.J. Andrews Experimental Forest were gearing up for a summer of intensive studies. They had the perfect site for examining the flood's effects on ecosystems: the H.J. Andrews, the most measured and analyzed forest in the Pacific Northwest. The streams had been mapped, past logging operations had been recorded in detail, and there were databases on past stream flows. In Mack Creek, the pieces of large driftwood had been tagged, counted, and mapped, and even the cutthroat trout had been counted and fin-clipped. Now the postflood studies would gather data about the effects of the disturbance. There might not be another event like this for thirty years—about the length of most professional careers.

The scientists presented their initial findings at a workshop in October 1996. Roughly seventy people gathered at the forest headquarters near the town of Blue River. The group included foresters, biologists, and hydrologists. This time I wasn't the only writer. Several news reporters wanted to learn more about the connections between forests, floods, and streams.

The flood was a test of land management practices and scientific ideas. The researchers at the workshop were cautious. They talked about rough data and hypotheses. They hesitated to draw broad conclusions. But the data showed some clear trends.

The biggest question was, Did logging cause the flood? As background, the researchers had thirty years of data on logging and water yields from watersheds on the H.J. Andrews Forest and other western Oregon forests. In small watersheds with clear-cuts and roads, water discharge after rainstorms increased by 50 percent in the first five years after logging. Runoff after storms was still 25 to 40 percent higher in those same watersheds up to twenty-five years after logging had ended. Effects were harder to determine in larger watersheds. As best as could be measured, peak runoff increased by 10 to 15 percent for every 5 percent of the watershed cut. Runoff may have increased by as much as 100 percent in some watersheds. The forest roads were a major factor in the increase. They captured water draining off mountain slopes and routed it into ditches, through culverts, or directly down roads, channeling it into streams much faster than it would have traveled otherwise.

Logging didn't cause the February flood of 1996. Heavy rain on deep snow on frozen ground did. But logging amplified the flood's effects. In the H.J. Andrews, watersheds with clear-cuts had 14 to 60 percent higher runoff per unit of area than unlogged watersheds, even when the timber harvest had happened twenty to thirty years ago. Logging almost certainly increased the amount of water that drained off many watersheds in the Pacific Northwest. In heavily cut watersheds without flood control dams, the rivers probably crested higher than they would have otherwise, but there is no way to tell exactly how much higher.

However, most people lived in valleys below the dams, which held back huge volumes of water. In the Albany/Corvallis area of the Willamette Valley, the flood was roughly equivalent to a five-year flood before the dams and the intensive logging of the previous forty years. In most areas, it was not the record-breaking flood that some people claimed it to be.

Logging and roads amplified the flood's effects in another way—they increased landslides. The H.J. Andrews Forest had ninety-two slides. More sediment moved downstream in a few hours during the flood than in the previous thirty years. Larger slides scoured some headwater streams—the stair-step streams on the mountainsides—for long distances. When landslides hit the larger streams on valley floors, boulders and most trees stopped fairly quickly, but smaller rocks traveled farther. Together the slides and the flood reshaped the streams. New logjams piled up, old ones blew apart, new side channels were cut, and old ones were abandoned. Areas that were logged more than twenty years ago had fewer slides than recently cut areas, suggesting that the increased risk of landslides may begin to drop after twenty years, when young trees get larger.

Logging had one other big effect on streams—it minimized the refugia. Simplified streams had fewer places for life to survive the churning current. Stan Gregory, the Stream Team leader at Oregon State University, compared logjams in streams to seatbelts in cars. A seatbelt doesn't do anything until there's a wreck, but then it can save your life. Fish survived better in streams with a lot of large logs.

Cutthroat trout and Pacific giant salamanders survived the flood fairly well. In Mack Creek, Stan had found previously that typically about 30 percent of adult cutthroat trout live from one year to the next. In the summer of 1996, he found that 45 percent of the trout remained in the stream reach through old-growth forest, a little better than average. In the stream reach through a clear-cut, he observed only a 27 percent survival rate for the cutthroat: a little worse than average, but not devastating. Pacific giant salamanders had declined about 30 percent. Sculpins and dace, fish that live near stream bottoms, had been hit hard by the flood. Sculpins were down to about half of their previous numbers, and only 10 to 20 percent of dace had survived.

In every stream that had had fish before the flood, some fish survived, no matter how badly the stream had been damaged. Stan predicted that in five to ten years, their numbers would increase dramatically. For the aquatic insect larvae—the mayflies, stoneflies, and caddisflies—he estimated complete recovery in just one or two years. As fish and other biota recovered from their losses, they would benefit from the structural changes in the streams. The flood had cleaned silt from the gravels, carried new logs into the stream, flushed organic matter into the water, and created new habitats where it had reshaped the streams.

"These systems are tougher than we think," he said. "It's the very nature of these streams to be disturbed. These ecosystems have evolved to handle these types of floods. It's the urban areas, the synthetic chemicals and the concrete channels, that are outside the system's experience. This is where you find systems at one end of the spectrum, so nuked that they can't respond."

Stan used the word *nuked* casually. It could just as well have been *devastated*. But in fact, at least one river in the Pacific Northwest has literally been nuked—the Columbia.

Chapter 7

Uncoupling an Ecosystem

E verything in a watershed eventually works its way down to the river, whether it's gold flakes crumbling from a quartz outcropping or paint thinner poured out in a backyard after the paintbrushes are cleaned. The Tao Te Ching says, "The great rivers and seas are kings of all mountain streams because they skillfully stay below them. That is why they can be their kings." As they move through the lowest places on the landscape, rivers collect everything that is hidden and unseen in the watershed and eventually make it visible. The deepest secrets are revealed in the lowest places and the humblest creatures.

THE LOWER COLUMBIA RIVER

I am on the boat *Shamrock* near the mouth of the Pacific Northwest's greatest river, the Columbia. Tiki Charters is taking me and eleven other passengers on a day-long trip along the Inside Channel of the Columbia estuary. The lower Columbia has lost over half of its tidal swamps, marshes, and wetlands since the 1880s. The former marshes have been diked, drained, and turned into pastures and fields.

Near Astoria, where this boat tour started, the river is four miles wide. Above Tongue Point, it is seven miles wide. The shipping channel is near the Washington shore. Along the Oregon shoreline is an intricate network of low islands, tidal marshes and swamps, and mudflats. Narrow channels weave in and out among the islands. The skipper tells us that many of the channels are too shallow for even smaller boats like ours, and local knowledge is important for picking a safe route. Large parts of the islands are tidal marshes inundated at high tide, leaving about one foot of green marsh

Wildlife refuges protect this Sitka spruce swamp in the lower Columbia River, but refuge boundaries can't protect wildlife from contaminants such as DDT, dioxins, and PCBs in the river water. (Val Rapp)

grass emerging above the surface. I see a couple of great blue herons, some cormorants, and a lot of gulls. Much of what looks like open water is only a few inches deep over the ugly, but biologically productive, mudflats. Looking over to the shore, on the far side of the dikes, I see dairy cows grazing on pastures that are below the level of the river.

Along the channel from Svensen to Knappa, island ground slightly higher than the marshes and mudflats is covered by Sitka spruce swamps. Along with the spruce, the swamps are forested with cedars, hemlocks, alders, and dense thickets of willow. The understory is a tangle of brush. Small islands of marsh grass partially block the entrance to Blind Slough, which winds back into the swamps from the main channel. Small, weathered houses, old docks, and rotting pilings are the only remaining signs of the onetime river communities, which depended on the steamboats for mail, groceries, and transportation. Most of the buildings look deserted, although roads now reach a few spots on the shore. Farther up the estuary, houseboats are moored in a couple of sloughs.

The September day is overcast and the wind has picked up. The rest of the passengers have retreated to the cabin, and I am alone on the deck on the front bow. I button, zip, and pull my warm clothes around me and peer into the wind, watching the marshes and sloughs for bald eagles and thinking about the sad story of the Columbia estuary.

Much has been done to conserve the lower Columbia's remaining habitat. Lewis and Clark National Wildlife Refuge protects thirty-five thousand acres of islands, bars, mudflats, and tidal marshes along the Oregon shore. The smaller Julia Butler Hansen National Wildlife Refuge on the Washington side shelters another forty-four hundred acres, and The Nature Conservancy's Blind Slough Swamp protects close to another thousand acres. Filling wetlands or diking off new areas is prohibited now. With all that's been done, I find it heartbreaking that the fish and fish-eating wildlife—bald eagles, otters, mink, cormorants—of the lower Columbia are poisoned by toxins in the river water and mud, and that the refuge boundaries can't keep these contaminants out.

The fish-eating wildlife of the lower Columbia River are accumulating dioxins, PCBs (polychlorinated biphenyls), DDT (dichloro-diphenyl-trichloro-ethane) and its derivative DDE (dichloro-diphenyl-trichloro-ethylene), and heavy metals in their bodies. These substances are not present in great enough quantities to kill the animals. Instead, the toxins accumulate in their livers, are stored in their body fat, affect their ability to reproduce, and disrupt normal sexual development in the young, at least in male otters.

THE LEGACY

By the middle of the twentieth century, water quality was becoming a significant public concern in the Pacific Northwest. Over a period of 150 years, the pristine rivers and estuaries had been turned into channels awash with sewage and industrial wastes. A federal government report in 1951 found Puget Sound to be the sixth most polluted area in the United States. Pulp and paper mills poured untreated wastes into the sound and other Pacific Northwest waters. Fishermen were the first to pressure government to regulate the dumping, but there was strong resistance, based on fears that the mills would close rather than clean up.

Oregon's State Sanitary Authority, created in 1938, made little progress in cleaning up the Willamette River until after the end of World War II in 1945. Then the cities along the Willamette moved ahead with plans for the required primary sewage treatment facilities. The two smaller communities of Junction City and Newberg were the first to get their treatment plants on-line. By 1957, all cities on the river had complied except for Portland, but the bacterial contamination and lack of dissolved oxygen were still just as bad during the summer low flow. However, as the dams in the upper Willamette watershed became operational in the 1950s and 1960s, summer water levels nearly doubled in the lower river, thanks to releases from the reservoirs, and the first water quality improvements were measured.

The State Sanitary Authority next required pulp and paper mills to develop facilities to treat sulfite waste liquids and to stop dumping wood fiber sludge into the river, as these two waste products caused most of the oxygen depletion. By 1969, all mills along the Willamette River had installed primary treatment plants and were required to have secondary treatment in place by 1972. In the 1960s, cities were required to build secondary sewage treatment plants.

In 1968, after years of gradual improvement, the Willamette met water quality standards for dissolved oxygen, bacterial contamination, and temperature all the way down to Newberg, a few miles upstream from Portland. The next year, the entire river met the requirements, from its headwaters to its confluence with the Columbia. The level of dissolved oxygen in Portland harbor met standards for the first time since 1934.

A state law passed in 1967 authorized the creation of the Willamette River park system. At first, the goal was to create a greenway along both riverbanks from Dexter Dam above Eugene to the Columbia, a distance of 255 river miles. From Dexter Dam to the Willamette's headwaters, the river was bordered mostly by national forest land. This pioneering idea would have been the first deliberate creation of a protected riparian corridor along the entire length of a river. Although the greenway was planned more to meet recreational needs than to take care of biological needs, it would have given the river ecosystem some important protection. The original concept was later scaled down to a park system and resulted in many state and county parks and boat landings along the Willamette.

The people of Oregon were justifiably proud of how they had restored a river's vitality. Fish didn't have to hold their breath through Portland harbor any more. Similar cleanups were accomplished or under way for other rivers and estuaries in the Pacific Northwest. Dumping sewage or wood fiber pulp into a river was no longer an acceptable way to do business in the Pacific Northwest.

But people had barely begun to face the pollution problems of their rivers. They had dealt with only a few gross indicators of degraded water

When the effluent is cleaned up, the affluent move to the riverfront. These upscale condominiums are along the Willamette River in Portland. (Gene Skrine)

quality. Regulatory officials had not stopped the excessive amounts of fine sediments coming into rivers from land uses or lowered the elevated water temperatures in many smaller streams. The officials were just beginning to recognize the subtler degradation of water quality caused by industrial chemicals.

DDT was first used in World War II as an insecticide. In the following years, it was sprayed on crops, fields, forests, and swamps throughout the world, wherever people wanted large numbers of insects killed. DDT's devastating environmental effects were first revealed to the public by Rachel Carson in her book *Silent Spring,* published in 1962.

Once in the environment, DDT eventually breaks down to a substance called DDE, which persists for many years and is responsible for the reproductive problems associated with the pesticide. DDE enters the food chain, and animals can't eliminate it from their bodies once they absorb it. The chemical grows more concentrated as it moves up trophic levels— as smaller fish are eaten by bigger fish, and bigger fish are eaten by eagles.

As higher-level predators accumulate larger amounts of DDE in their bodies, they begin to have reproductive dysfunctions. In birds, the chemical interferes with calcium metabolism, causing thinning or softening of their eggshells. In the 1960s, DDE was a major cause of the population crashes of top raptors, such as bald eagles, osprey, and peregrine falcons.

The United States banned DDT in 1972, except for use in health emergencies, such as a malaria outbreak. Most other organochlorine pesticides have also been banned in this country, although some are still used elsewhere.

Dioxins are generally unwanted by-products of various industrial processes. In the Pacific Northwest, dioxins are created most often by pulp and paper mills, in the process of bleaching paper to make it white. The notorious herbicide 2,4,5-T, best known for its use in Agent Orange in the Vietnam War, contains dioxin, and was used in some Pacific Northwest forests to kill deciduous trees growing in conifer plantations. It was banned in the United States in 1979. Pulp and paper mills in the Northwest are slowly adopting a new process that greatly reduces the amount of dioxin they produce. However, some dioxins are still being discharged into rivers.

PCBs were used in industrial production and as insulating fluid in electrical transformers and capacitors. They were banned in the United States in 1979.

Like DDT, dioxins and PCBs accumulate to greater and greater concentrations as they move up the food chain from plankton, through invertebrates such as snails and worms, to fish, and eventually to eagles, otters, and people. At the top of the food chain, toxic chemicals can be concentrated in body tissues by a factor of millions over the levels found in plankton or algae. Some species are more sensitive to toxic chemicals than others, and the various chemicals cause different results in different species. Effects include cancer, reproductive failure, reproductive abnormalities, and suppression of the immune system. Much is still unknown about exactly how these toxins cause their biological damage and what their long-term effects may be over generations.

During the 1970s and 1980s, researchers found evidence of toxic chemicals in lower Columbia wildlife. In 1970s tests, otters and mink along the lower river had the highest levels of PCBs yet recorded in North American wildlife. Mink are known to be particularly sensitive to PCBs and dioxins, and the PCB concentrations found in Columbia River mink exceeded levels known to cause total reproductive failure in the species.

Scientific evidence and concern over the health of the lower river grew through the 1980s. In 1990, to develop a comprehensive picture of pollution in the Columbia and its effects on wildlife and human health, Oregon and Washington started the Lower Columbia River Bi-State Program. Local and federal agencies and private interests cooperated with the states on the research. For reference levels of contaminants, the scientists used legal standards when these existed, and in situations where no legal standards had been set, they used available reference levels in the scientific literature. The program generated more than fifty technical reports in six years, culminating in the publication of its final report in 1996. The final document also included information on the loss and degradation of habitat in the lower Columbia, but the findings on contaminants presented stunning new information.

Although DDT was banned in 1972, its derivative DDE was still coming into the Yakima Basin, apparently through soil erosion from orchards heavily sprayed before the ban. From there, DDE traveled down the Columbia.

The lower Columbia River (from Bonneville Dam to the mouth) has had forty or more nesting pairs of bald eagles in recent years, and over a hundred bald eagles spend the winter in the estuary, where they have prime habitat and an abundance of food. Nevertheless, bald eagle nesting success in the estuary averages nearly 50 percent lower than statewide species averages in Oregon and Washington. Researchers found that levels of DDE, PCBs, and dioxins in lower Columbia eagles in 1994–95 were slightly lower than the levels measured in 1985–87, but that eagles and eagle eggs were still accumulating these contaminants at levels associated with reduced reproductive success. Eagle breeding success increased slightly from 1993 to 1995, although it was not clear whether the improvement was the result of lower contamination levels or if the arrival of new eagles from outside the area skewed the data toward positive results.

In the winter of 1994–95, the Bi-State Program contracted with licensed trappers to capture mink and otters along a hundred-mile stretch of the lower Columbia. Researchers analyzed the frozen animal carcasses for contaminants. The trappers took only two mink, whose contaminant levels were below threshold levels for serious effects. The Bi-State scientists suspected, but could not prove, that mink had died out along the lower Columbia, after failing to reproduce as a result of the high contaminant levels measured in the 1970s, and that the two trapped mink had recently traveled to the river from another area, attracted by the lower Columbia's plentiful fish and habitat.

Thirty river otters were trapped in the same hundred-mile study reach. When researchers tested the livers, kidneys, and body fat for contaminants, these otter tissues were found to contain high levels of DDE and other organochlorine insecticides, PCBs, and dioxins. All the young male otter specimens showed defects in their reproductive organs. Male otters have a thin bone called the baculum that supports the penis. In the young Columbia males, the baculum was significantly smaller than in otters from a reference area. Average testicle weight was also lower for the young Columbia male otters, and differences could be observed at the cellular level. The reproductive organs of older Columbia male otters were normal in size, suggesting that the problem might be a temporary developmental one. But as of early 1997, it was not known if young male otters from the lower Columbia would eventually develop normally and be able to reproduce.

The Bi-State Program report concluded that young male Columbia River otters showed underdevelopment of male reproductive organs that correlated most closely with the levels of organochlorine insecticides and PCBs in the otters' livers. These effects had been demonstrated in laboratory tests before, but had not been seen in free-living mammals. The lower Columbia otters were the first wild mammal population in North America to show this problem. It was not the sort of thing that the Pacific Northwest wanted to lead the nation in.

The highest levels of contaminants were found in four river otters collected near river mile 119.5, just above the Portland-Vancouver area, in the vicinity of a large aluminum refinery on the Oregon side and a pulp and paper mill on the Washington side. These four animals had also accumulated aluminum and lead, which were rare in the other otter specimens. Three of the four river-mile 119.5 otters had gross defects, including a missing kidney, a missing adrenal gland, and a large cystic abscess; one young male had no testicles at all.

The mink, otters, and eagles were getting these contaminants in the fish they ate. Additional study was done to assess the levels of toxins in Columbia River fish, and to determine the health risks to people eating these fish. Researchers tested carp, large-scale suckers, peamouths (a member of the carp and minnow family), white sturgeon, steelhead, coho salmon, and chinook salmon. As expected, they found the same contaminants as were in the fish-eating mammals and birds. Concentrations varied according to fish species. Reference levels for PCBs were exceeded frequently in the tested fish tissues, especially in whole-body samples of large-scale suckers and peamouths. The reference levels for dioxins were also exceeded fairly often in the fish specimens. The chinook, coho, and steelhead had much lower levels of the toxic chemicals since these fish had only recently returned to the river from the ocean.

In May 1996, the health departments of Oregon and Washington issued warnings about eating carp, peamouths, and large-scale suckers, the bottom-feeding fish that had the highest levels of contaminants. People—especially pregnant and nursing women, women planning to have children, and small children—were advised to limit their consumption of these fish, although recommendations were not given as to specific amounts. The health departments suggested reducing exposure by skinning the fish and removing the body fat before cooking, as most contaminants were concentrated in the fat. These fish were not popular with sports anglers, but Native Americans near the Columbia, who had turned to other fish since few salmon were available, were eating nine times as much fish as the general public. The Columbia River Intertribal Fish Commission planned to test the blood of tribal members for contaminants. Immigrant groups from Southeast Asia and Russia were also eating these fish. The health agencies posted signs in six languages at the Columbia Slough in Portland and other popular fishing spots.

The contaminant problems were not limited to the lower Columbia. In Seattle, the Duwamish Waterway flows past Harbor Island and into the south end of Elliott Bay. Researchers from the National Marine Fisheries Service found in 1986 that salmon smolts passing through the Duwamish picked up enough PCBs and other toxins to partially suppress their immune systems, making them more vulnerable to disease. The exposed fish had reduced growth rates compared with smolts from less urban estuaries, such as those of the Nisqually and Skykomish Rivers. Contaminants were also affecting bottom-dwelling fish in the Duwamish, such as starry flounders and English sole. Hormone levels in female fish were altered, delaying spawning, and some male fish had traces of a protein associated with egg production.

Other researchers started checking local rivers for contaminants in fish and wildlife. The Oregon Department of Environmental Quality began a study of toxins in Willamette River fish in the early 1990s. The project was still under way in early 1997, but some findings had already been reported. Researchers found an overall fish deformity rate of about 3 percent in the Willamette between Eugene and Portland. Most deformities were minor, but some data were troubling. Out of twenty suckers collected, four were missing one or both eyes. The abnormalities appeared to be birth defects, rather than the result of disease or injury. In a river

These Native American women were drying salmon along the Columbia River in the 1950s. As salmon runs declined, some Native Americans turned to other types of fish. Recent studies found these fish may pose a health risk due to dioxins and PCBs accumulated in their bodies. (photo courtesy Oregon Historical Society, OrHi 60409, Oregon State Highway Commission photo)

reach between Eugene and Springfield, 80 percent of fish sampled had damaged or deformed gills. Near the lower end of the river, where water pollution had been heavy over the years, squawfish in a thirty-five-mile stretch between Newberg and Willamette Falls had a skeletal deformity rate ranging from 22 to 74 percent. The causes of the various deformities had not yet been determined as of the time of this writing, and it is possible that parasites or other factors in addition to contaminants could have been responsible for some of the defects seen.

Pollutants get into water in three ways: from point sources (discharges directly into rivers through pipes); in-place sources (landfills, hazardous waste sites, or other sources that leak into groundwater); and nonpoint sources (water runoff from farmlands, city streets, and other lands). The

Willamette River cleanup of the 1960s had focused on point sources—discharges from industrial plants, sewage treatment plants, or other identifiable sites. It had largely succeeded. The 1990s study found that nonpoint sources now contributed 70 to 80 percent of the river's pollution. Only 0.5 percent of particulate matter—actual particles—came from point sources. The other 99.5 percent originated from nonpoint sources. (Contributions from in-place sources were not analyzed in this study.) Just four sub-basins contributed most of the Willamette's pollution: the Pudding, Tualatin, Long Tom, and Yamhill-Luckiamute. The Pudding contributed the most, primarily from farmlands. It was time for Oregonians to stop congratulating themselves on the successful river cleanup of the 1960s and to look at their rivers again.

THE HANFORD REACH

While scientists in New Mexico worked to develop the first atomic bombs, the Hanford Nuclear Reservation, a 640-square-mile site along the Columbia River in central Washington, was created to manufacture plutonium for the bombs.

Starting in March 1943, in just twenty-nine months, the United States military, with the help of thousands of civilian workers, built the town of Richland and the initial Hanford nuclear facility, and produced enough plutonium for two nuclear bombs. The two devices were the world's first nuclear bomb, exploded in New Mexico in July 1945, and the atomic bomb dropped on Nagasaki in August 1945 that ended World War II. Three nuclear reactors were constructed in World War II, and five more were added between 1947 and 1955 as Hanford continued to be a critical facility in the U.S. nuclear weapons program during the Cold War.

The presence of the nuclear reservation initially saved the Hanford Reach as the last free-flowing stretch of the Columbia, for the construction of a large dam near the plutonium-producing facilities was considered a security risk. Also, the reactors used vast amounts of water for cooling, and a free-flowing river was needed to quickly dilute the radioactive wastewater before it got to the tri-cities of Richland, Kennewick, and Pasco downriver.

Most of Hanford Nuclear Reservation was in a large block west of the Columbia, but a strip of land along the east bank, known as the Wahluke Slope, was included as a buffer. The plutonium reactors released radioactive emissions into the air as well as into the water, and the predominant winds were from the west. The Wahluke Slope was exposed to the worst of the airborne emissions and was kept in the reservation so it would stay uninhabited. The large plateau farther east was developed into farmlands. By keeping the Hanford Reach free-flowing and the riparian corridor in a natural state, the military inadvertently created a wildlife refuge.

As the only free-flowing stretch of the Columbia, the Hanford Reach is the part of the river most similar ecologically to the original, wild Columbia. It is a stronghold for fish and wildlife species that once ranged along most of the river. The reach has riffles, gravel bars, oxbow ponds, sloughs, backwaters, cobble shorelines, islands, and forested wetlands on the floodplain—habitats that were common along the Columbia before the dams but which are now rare.

The Hanford Reach has the only fall chinook spawning areas left in the Columbia River, and white sturgeon also spawn here. The shortface lanx and the Columbia pebblesnail are two freshwater snails that used to be common throughout the Columbia and Snake Rivers. Both species need unpolluted, swift-flowing, highly oxygenated water and a riverbed of boulders and gravel. Both are now gone from most of their original range but are found in the Hanford Reach. Fish species live here that are becoming scarce in other places: mountain sucker, sandroller, paiute sculpin, and reticulate sculpin. Bald eagles, peregrine falcons, and white pelicans use the river and uplands. The reach offers badly needed refuge to many species but exposes them to the unique hazards coming from the nuclear reservation.

Scientists already knew in the 1940s that radioactivity was dangerous, but they didn't know how much waste they would produce, how to dispose of it, how it would travel in the environment, how radioactivity would concentrate in the food chain, and what the biomedical effects would be of less-than-lethal amounts of radiation. The program was a rush one that demanded immediate results. Radioactive substances were entering the air, water, and ground as soon as operations started at Hanford, and scientists learned the consequences through experience.

River monitoring started in 1943. The nuclear reactors created three water pollution problems. The first was thermal pollution. Millions of gallons of river water were used to cool the reactors, and warm water flowing back into the river raised the river temperature. Second was the chemicals added to the cooling water. By 1964, reactor effluent carried roughly fifty thousand tons of chemicals per year, primarily sulfates, into the Columbia. The third problem was the radioactive isotopes carried in the water. In order to let the short-lived isotopes decay, the reactor effluent was held in basins before being released to the river, but by 1960 the holding time was only three hours, or even less.

The river did not flush the radioactivity downstream as rapidly as scientists had hoped. Effluent tended to channel in the river instead of dispersing evenly through the water. Sometimes it formed "bubbles" around release points. Some isotopes adhered to particulates on the river bottom. As the sediments recirculated, the isotopes did too.

When Hanford started plutonium production, scientists did not understand the way radioactivity concentrated in living tissues as it moved up the food chain. As they monitored the radioactivity in the river, they found that algae concentrated the radiation from the water by a factor of a thousand and that bottom-dwelling animals concentrated it by a factor of up to twenty-three hundred. By 1947, only a few years after the nuclear program began, scientists detected radioactivity in fish livers, kidneys, and gills concentrated up to a hundred thousand times the level present in the river water.

The radioactivity levels in Hanford Reach game fish continued to rise through the 1950s. By 1958, biologists calculated that if a person ate one pound per week of Hanford Reach whitefish, he or she would reach the maximum permissible level of P-32, the phosphorus radioisotope. Waterfowl along the Hanford Reach posed a similar risk. Hanford scientists discussed closing fishing in the reach, but no closures occurred. Despite the findings, no warnings were issued to people fishing in the reach or hunting ducks along the east bank. Throughout the 1950s and 1960s, as effluent releases reached their highest level, scientists assured the public that the radioactivity dosages they would get from eating local fish would be well within permissible levels.

Mitigation for thermal pollution didn't begin until 1957. Then a program was initiated that released cold water from the bottom of Lake Roosevelt (the reservoir behind Grand Coulee Dam) in late summer and fall to cool water downstream in Hanford Reach.

Production levels rose in the eight plutonium-producing reactors from 1956 to 1963. The reactors closed down between 1964 and 1971 as the military's need for plutonium dropped. As production ended, the amount of warm water entering the river dropped sharply, and the cold-water release program was discontinued. Radioactivity in the river also declined considerably after the closures, although some isotopes remained in the sediments and river life. The mid-Columbia salmon runs declined significantly in the 1950s, when plutonium production was at its highest levels. Although it is not known what role pollution from Hanford played in the population declines, salmon runs increased somewhat in the late 1960s as plutonium production dropped.

By then, a new water pollution problem was emerging. Since 1945, liquid wastes with low levels of radioactivity had been discharged into the ground away from the river through dry wells, cribs, and tile fields. The radioactive particles in this waste were longer lived than the particles in the reactor effluent but were expected to decay and disappear by the time the groundwater reached the Columbia or Yakima Rivers.

In the five-year period from 1951 to 1955, approximately 20 billion gallons of low-level waste were poured into the ground. From 1956 to 1960, another 32 billion gallons were dumped. When these enormous volumes of liquid were discharged into ground that normally got about eight inches of rain a year, they changed the groundwater flow patterns dramatically. First the wastes created "mounds" of groundwater. Then they pushed the groundwater to a faster rate of flow and even changed the direction of its course.

In 1960, Hanford hydrologists predicted that waste-contaminated groundwater would take at least 175 years to reach the two rivers. By 1963, contaminated plumes of groundwater were within one mile of the Columbia. By 1964, tritium-contaminated groundwater had reached the river. (Tritium is a radioactive substance, and the contamination was in concentrations above safe drinking water standards.) No one knew how to stop it. Over the next thirty years, the plume spread into a wider, fan-like shape along an ever greater part of the Columbia's west bank. By 1993, tritium-contaminated groundwater was draining into the Columbia along roughly one-third of the Hanford Reach.

Highly radioactive nuclear wastes and hazardous chemicals were stored in underground storage tanks. Leaks from these tanks were first confirmed in 1956. By 1995, sixty-seven tanks were known to have leaked, or suspected of having leaked, high-level wastes into the soil. The three largest spills released 115,000, 70,000, and 55,000 gallons of these wastes into the ground. Most hazardous materials from the older, single-shelled storage tanks have now been transferred into new, double-walled tanks, but little progress has been made on actually cleaning up the stored and leaked substances. I have not seen any information on whether or not these high-level wastes are reaching, or are expected to reach, the river.

An attempt was made in the 1960s and 1970s to turn Hanford into a civilian powerhouse that would rival Columbia dams in electricity production. A consortium of public utilities from the region established the

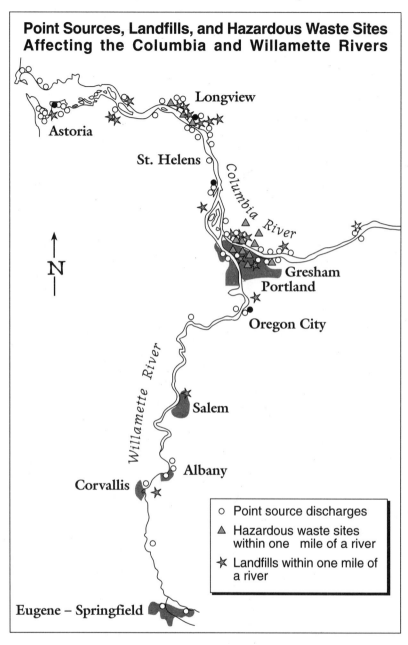

Point Sources, Landfills, and Hazardous Waste Sites Affecting the Columbia and Willamette Rivers

Longview

Astoria

St. Helens

Columbia River

N

Gresham
Portland

Oregon City

Willamette River

Salem

Albany

Corvallis

○ Point source discharges

▲ Hazardous waste sites
within one mile of a river

✸ Landfills within one mile of
a river

Eugene – Springfield

This map shows point sources and in-place sources of pollution along the lower Columbia and Willamette Rivers. All point sources have permits and their discharge is legal. Locations of pollution sources are approximate, and information on the Willamette River is incomplete.

Washington Public Power Supply System (WPPSS) project, with plans for five nuclear power plants to be built at Hanford. One plant went on-line in 1966 and is still producing electricity today. Construction began on two more power plants, but because of cost overruns, high interest rates, and falling power demand, these plants were never completed, and plans for the remaining two were canceled. WPPSS ended up billions of dollars in debt, defaulted on bonds sold to finance the project, and was left with one nuclear power plant in operation.

The National Park Service recommended in 1994 that the Hanford Reach be designated a wild and scenic river and the east bank a national wildlife refuge, both to be administered by the U.S. Fish and Wildlife Service. Commissioners of the four local counties would rather see most of the land sold to farmers, keeping some for a county-managed scenic river and wildlife refuge. As of early 1997, no decisions had been made. No land from Hanford Nuclear Reservation had been redesignated to other uses. The northern end of the east bank is now the Saddle Mountain National Wildlife Refuge, managed under special permit with the U.S. Department of Energy. The central and southern parts of the strip are managed by the Washington Department of Wildlife as the Wahluke Wildlife Area.

I don't know what to expect when Gene and I visit the Wahluke Slope on a sunny, warm October day. Across the river, the WPPSS reactor has steam coming from its cooling towers. The plumes are a clean white against a brilliant blue sky. On our way down to the river, a sign warns us to evacuate the area if we hear a siren that stays on for three minutes.

I can't quite forget about the three-minute warning siren. But I almost forget, because the Columbia River is so beautiful here. The water is clear and blue, and the current is strong. Fishermen drifting in their boats float quickly by us while we watch from the shore. Families are camping on the bank. Most of the shore is cobbles, but in one muddy stretch I see raccoon tracks. Ducks and geese are resting on low islands covered with straw-colored grasses. A half dozen white pelicans wheel above the river. They are a brilliant white against the blue sky, even whiter

Source of map, opposite: Based on maps from *The Health of the River, 1990–1996: Integrated Technical Reports,* by Tetra Tech, Inc., for the Columbia River Bi-State Water Quality Program. Also used as a reference: *Portland/Vancouver Toxic Waters,* map prepared by Columbia–Willamette River Watch, a program of Northwest Environment Advocates, 1992.

than the steam plumes, with striking black bands on their wing tips.

Nearby we find Ringold Springs. Fresh spring water emerges from the base of a chalk-colored hillside in dozens of places. A sign honors Lowell Johnson, a sportsman and conservationist who lived from 1907 to 1980. After plutonium production declined at Hanford, the proposal to dam the river and turn this last reach into a reservoir resurfaced. But, along with organizations that he often led—the Northwest Steelheaders, the Columbia River Conservation League, and the Washington State Sportsmen's Council—Johnson fought to keep the Hanford Reach free-flowing. The proposed construction of Ben Franklin Dam was halted in 1969.

The river feels alive and beautiful here. Gene and I walk through fields of tall grasses mixed with groves of cottonwoods and Russian olives. I hear a lot of birds, but I can't identify them. I sit down in the sun to rewrite my notes.

Yesterday Gene and I visited the northern end of Wahluke Wildlife Area. We drove across a flat plateau crisscrossed by irrigation canals. The farms had apple orchards and fields of alfalfa, carrots, potatoes, and asparagus. From the northern end of the wildlife area we could see the line of old, shut-down nuclear reactors along the river's west bank. Long bands of gray clouds stretched across the sky parallel to the distant ridges of the Rattlesnake Hills and the nearby gray stripe of the Columbia. At dusk, the sun started to drop behind the hills, and the clouds just above the ridges turned a soft pink. A crescent moon shone in the narrow strip of indigo sky between the gray clouds above and the pink horizon below. Ducks flew by, then a great blue heron.

Gene commented on the contrast between the scale of the mountains; the plain, big sky and big river; and the old plutonium-producing reactors. The concrete buildings actually looked small in this landscape. "We thought we could contain and control things here because it seemed simple," he said. "But it wasn't simple. As soon as we started intruding, things became infinitely more complex."

THE GIFT

The generative link between parents and children is perhaps the single most important connection in society and ecosystems. If it breaks once, that lineage is gone. So far, no evidence has been found that human beings are having contaminant-caused reproductive disorders similar to the problems found in the mink and otters of the lower Columbia River. But if contaminant levels get high enough in people, the same problems could develop.

Typically, the effects of toxic chemicals show up first in more subtle ways. Fish and fish-eating wildlife in the Great Lakes have also suffered from contaminant-caused disorders. When researchers studied people who ate a lot of fish from Lake Michigan, they found that these people's children had lesser cognitive abilities, poorer memory, and shorter attention spans when compared with a control group.

No studies have been done yet on people who eat a lot of fish from the lower Columbia River, or their children. The otters and mink have made the unseen contaminants visible. Thanks to them, perhaps we have enough time to respond before genetic damage uncouples our ecosystems and cuts the links between our own generations.

The gift of the Columbia River otters and mink is the advance warning.

Chapter 8

The Landscape of Salmon

You hear the river saying a prayer for all that's gone.
William Stafford, "The Methow River Poems"

T he most striking characteristic of the landscape of salmon is how fast it's shrinking.

Wherever Western civilization has come, wild salmon have dwindled or disappeared. The only places where they coexist are places where we have just recently come. We hope Oregon is the place where we can turn this trend around and prove that salmon and Western civilization can coexist.

The speaker, Jim Martin, from the Oregon Department of Fish and Wildlife, is talking to a group of foresters in Eugene about his assignment for Oregon governor John Kitzhaber—to lead a team in developing a restoration plan for coho salmon.

He is not alone. Many of us throughout the Pacific Northwest want to prove that salmon and Western civilization can live together, that people and nature can be reconciled. Perhaps here computer chip factories and clean rivers, lumber mills and coho salmon, white paper and bald eagles can live together.

The wild salmon have the public's attention and love in a way the spotted owl never did. People turn out to watch when the salmon come through Seattle's Chittenden Locks on their way into Lake Washington and its tributaries. A steady stream of families, young couples, and older people moves along the walkways that follow the zigzagging fish ladder. In the glass-walled viewing room that allows visitors to watch the migrating fish underwater, parents hold children on their shoulders so the kids can see the salmon. The annual Wenatchee River Salmon Festival in Leavenworth has gotten bigger every year. The return of the chinook and sockeye is celebrated with three days of "salmon edu-tainment." Salmon jewelry, salmon T-shirts, and smoked salmon fillets (which by 1997 were mostly Alaskan salmon) sell well throughout the region. The more endangered the salmon get, the more popular they are with the public, at least as an icon.

When the National Marine Fisheries Service (NMFS) listed three Snake River salmon stocks as threatened and endangered species in 1991 and 1992, it was big news in the Pacific Northwest for two reasons. First, it was a decision that individual salmon stocks could be protected, under the clause of the Endangered Species Act that allowed "evolutionarily significant units" of species to be listed. Second, fish biologists and agency managers believed that more salmon were in trouble than just those three stocks. Depending on your point of view, more salmon listings would be either an economic disaster for the region, or the canary-in-the-mineshaft that would save regional ecosystems.

THE CROSSROADS

Roughly at the same time the Snake River salmon were listed, a magazine article in a professional journal provided the first comprehensive survey of the status of Pacific salmon stocks. In the March–April 1991 issue of *Fisheries,* the American Fisheries Society published an article called "Pacific Salmon at the Crossroads: Stocks at Risk from California, Oregon, Idaho, and Washington," written by Willa Nehlsen, Jack Williams, and Jim Lichatowich, three biologists well known among fisheries professionals in the Pacific Northwest. At the time of publication, two of the authors worked for federal agencies—Willa Nehlsen for the Northwest Power Planning Council and Jack Williams for the Bureau of Land Management; Jim Lichatowich worked as a fisheries consultant. At first only fish biologists saw the report. But the findings were widely reported in the region's newspapers and quickly became the focus of the growing discussion. "Crossroads" inventoried all native, naturally spawning salmon, steelhead, and sea-run cutthroat stocks on the Pacific Coast. In their survey, the authors found 214 stocks at risk. Out of the 214, almost half—101 stocks—were at high risk of extinction. The authors noted that 18 of the stocks might already be extinct. There was no doubt about others: they also listed 106 stocks of Pacific Coast salmon and steelhead known to be extinct.

The "Crossroads" article was the wake-up call. Snake River salmon that had to get past eight dams were not the only runs in trouble. The problem was regionwide and systemic. The salmon were in serious decline in rivers that didn't have any dams, like Oregon coastal rivers. Salmon were in trouble, and in fact they were often in the worst trouble, in rivers where large, expensive hatchery programs were operating.

Willa Nehlsen, now a consultant, explained to me that no one else had looked at salmon stocks on the entire Pacific coast. Fish biologists knew about the problems in their own areas, and they knew dams had hurt salmon runs in the Columbia River basin. Some biologists thought the declines in the late 1980s were caused by poor ocean conditions and that salmon would rebound when the ocean cycle changed. "I didn't have the same background as the other salmon biologists," Willa told me. "If I did, I wouldn't have done 'Crossroads.' It took an outsider to look at the broad view."

"We had no idea how far-reaching the problem was," she continued. "Only one environmental organization, Oregon Trout, considered salmon an issue in the eighties." "Crossroads" was instrumental to the recognition of salmon as a significant environmental concern.

The public responded by writing letters to their representatives and forming new organizations like Save Our Salmon. Jim Lichatowich told me, "People said, 'We care about wild salmon and we want you to do something about it.' The surprise to me was that so many people felt that way."

The salmon crisis grew through the 1990s. NMFS had listed Snake River spring/summer chinook and fall chinook as threatened species in 1992, but two years later the agency proposed to change the species' status to "endangered" as their numbers continued to drop. (The Snake River sockeye had already been designated as endangered when it was listed in 1991.) Other species were proposed for listing: Umpqua River sea-run cutthroat trout, Klamath Mountains steelhead, coho populations. Finally, NMFS announced in 1994 that they would review the status of all Pacific salmon and anadromous trout in Washington, Oregon, Idaho, and California.

The Oregon coastal coho salmon were already crashing when I went to the Pacific Rivers Council workshop on the Siuslaw River in 1994. A little more than a year later, NMFS proposed to list the central California coho, southern Oregon/northern California coho, and Oregon coast coho populations as threatened species.

In early 1997, after taking public comments, NMFS listed the central California coho as a threatened species. But they delayed a decision on the Oregon coho populations while the state of Oregon worked on an unusual response. Oregon governor John Kitzhaber wanted to use a provision of the federal Endangered Species Act that had rarely been applied before. The law provides that if a state government can develop a viable recovery plan for the species in question, the federal government can decide not to list the species, allowing the state to take charge of recovery without federal intervention. If Oregon could avoid a listing, it would prevent the economic costs and social conflicts that resulted when the spotted owl was listed at the beginning of the 1990s. Jim Martin was leading the team developing the coho recovery plan, and he was out getting support from the groups who would make the proposal work—foresters, farmers, and fishermen, among others.

By March 1997, the state of Oregon had developed its coho recovery plan and presented it to NMFS. On April 25, 1997, NMFS announced their decision: they would not list the Oregon coastal coho, and would accept the state's recovery plan for these stocks. The agency did list the southern Oregon/northern California coho, a decision that applied to the southernmost sixty miles of Oregon's coastline. Oregon state officials were pleased that their restoration proposal was accepted for the majority of Oregon's coastal rivers. They viewed it as a new approach to the Endangered Species Act—restoring species and their habitats through a homegrown strategy and voluntary efforts, instead of through top-down intervention by the federal government. Clinton administration officials saw their decision as a demonstration of their willingness to be flexible and let states come up with innovative solutions. One official referred to it as a "watershed event," with no apparent intention of irony.

Outside government, the reaction was mixed. A coalition of twenty-five environmental groups said they might go to court to challenge the decision not to list. The timber industry supported the state plan, and pledged to provide $15 million annually for the next ten years for restoration projects—a lot more money than the spotted owl ever got from timber companies. "Save the salmon!" was turning out to be an idea that people rallied around enthusiastically.

Can salmon and Western civilization live together in the Pacific Northwest? These men were seining for salmon on the Columbia River, circa 1920. (photo courtesy Oregon Historical Society, Gi 7185, Ben Gifford photo)

OCEAN CYCLES AND SALMON

Salmon runs always had a lot of variation. The historic Columbia River runs were estimated to vary from 10 to 16 million fish each year. Runs fluctuated depending on conditions in their home watersheds, and they also varied over long-term cycles that are still only partially understood.

The ocean currents are rivers that dwarf the Columbia. Global climate patterns affect the circulation of these massive currents—or perhaps the ocean currents influence global climate patterns. Scientists aren't completely sure. Whichever it is, ocean currents and climate fluctuate in twenty- to sixty-year cooling and warming cycles. The northern Pacific Ocean had a warming period from roughly 1925 to 1947, then a cooling trend until 1976, followed by another warming period that showed signs of ending in 1996. The warm parts of the cycles have been associated with droughts in the Pacific Northwest, and the cool parts with higher rainfall and cooler temperatures.

The ocean current off the Washington and Oregon coasts fluctuates along with the climate cycles. In the cool parts of the long-term cycles, cold, nutrient-rich water upwells off the coast every summer, coming from deeper ocean levels. Plankton blooms thrive and feed a rich food chain, including the millions of small fish that growing salmon feed on. During the warm parts of the long-term cycles, shifts in ocean currents delay and weaken the yearly upwelling. Deprived of nutrients from the ocean depths, the plankton dwindle, the food chain collapses, and with less food, the numbers of fish drop. In 1996, the summer upwelling didn't begin until July instead of late spring. When the numbers of small fish plummeted, an estimated ten thousand murres, a common seabird, starved off the coast of Oregon, where they nest every summer. Pacific Northwest salmon do best during the cool parts of the long-term cycles, and like the murres, have trouble finding enough food during the warm parts of the cycles.

Changes in ocean conditions can cause salmon populations to vary by as much as a factor of ten. Most things that fish biologists do only influence salmon numbers by a factor of two to three, less than the natural variation. So it is incredibly difficult to separate the signal from the noise with salmon—to separate significant population trends from the static of normal fluctuations.

We have usually believed the salmon theory that was most convenient at the time. When more fish came back in the 1960s, most fishery managers believed it was their improved hatchery practices that caused the change. Only a few biologists suggested that it was favorable ocean conditions, not our good deeds. When fewer fish came back during the 1980s and early 1990s, many people blamed it on unfavorable ocean conditions. We wanted to believe that it wasn't our fault.

Salmon have always dealt with the ups and downs of ocean cycles. But they always depended on the freshwater streams as their refuge, the stronghold that enabled them to survive. For the last 150 years, people have degraded streams and rivers throughout the Pacific Northwest, and inevitably the widespread damage affected salmon survival. Biologist Pete Lawson developed the following graph, which shows how ocean cycles and habitat degradation together have affected coho salmon. In the past, the coho population stayed reasonably strong even at low points on the cycle. But the worsening condition of freshwater streams and rivers has caused a long downhill slide. The high points were lower each time through the cycle, and the low points dropped to new lows. The degradation of freshwater habitat controlled the long-term decline of coho salmon.

Although the graph was developed for coho, the general principle applies to all salmon and seagoing trout. Juvenile coho spend one or two years in freshwater. Salmon species that spend less time in freshwater, like fall chinook, have not been as strongly affected by the degradation of freshwater streams and rivers.

The graph leaves out one critical factor: fish harvest. Government agencies that regulate fishing have been widely criticized for not reducing

Ocean Cycles, Freshwater Habitat, and the Decline of Coho Salmon

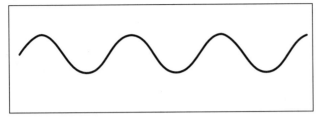

Part A: Ocean Conditions

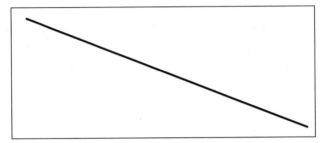

Part B: Freshwater Habitat Quality

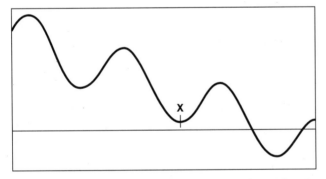

Part C: The Result – The Two Factors Combined

Twenty- to sixty-year cycles in ocean conditions affect ocean food chains and salmon survival in the ocean (Part A). Human activities have steadily degraded freshwater habitat over time (Part B). Both factors influence coho salmon, and the result is the trend seen in Part C. Temporary upswings in ocean conditions can mask the long-term trend of coho decline. Many fish biologists believe that Point X on Part C of the graph marks the point reached in the early 1990s. The next downturn could result in the extinction of threatened stocks, unless freshwater habitat is restored.

harvest rates enough on declining salmon runs. Too often, fish management agencies poured hatchery fish into rivers instead, and then kept harvest rates high. The fishing pressure made it impossible for salmon to recover from the low points of the cycle.

By the early 1990s, we had reached the point marked x on part C of the graph. Salmon populations had gotten so low that most commercial salmon fishing was finally prohibited off much of the Pacific Northwest coast. Ocean conditions seemed to be swinging back toward the up side of the cycle by 1997. But many biologists feared that fish management agencies would raise fishing levels immediately. Jim Lichatowich commented:

As soon as there's a little increase, people want to increase harvest right away. How people can think we should do this is beyond me. I feel sorry for the fishermen, just like I do the loggers, but the fact is it is in their best interest to let these populations grow.

The other danger was that people would think the salmon crisis was over and forget about restoring rivers. If river ecosystems weren't healed, we would see the sad result in twenty years. When ocean cycles dropped into their next trough, the salmon stocks that fell so low in the 1990s would drop to zero the next time—extinction.

Jim Martin said, "It took us thirty years to get into this mess, and it'll take us thirty years to get out. But the first time ocean conditions turn around, everybody will be high-fiving." He was wrong about one thing, though. It actually took us closer to two hundred years to get into this mess.

THE RIVER HEALTH CRISIS

The landscape of salmon and steelhead used to be the entire Pacific coast from Mexico to Alaska, and around the Alaskan coast to the Arctic Ocean. Salmon used to migrate up tributaries of the Snake River into Nevada and the Owyhee River in southeastern Oregon. They made it to the Stanley Basin lakes high in Idaho's Sawtooth Mountains. In the 1800s, winter steelhead returned to the San Diego and Los Angeles Rivers. Most larger streams in southern California had steelhead runs that varied from five thousand to twenty thousand fish annually. Now, the only

Source of graph, opposite: Peter W. Lawson, National Marine Fisheries Service

oceangoing survivor of the southern California runs is a remnant steel-head population that spawns in Malibu Creek in Los Angeles County.

The "Crossroads" article had shown clearly, for the first time, how many Pacific Coast salmon stocks were at risk. The blanket of salmon was ragged and torn and barely holding together. Another biologist, Chris Frissell, analyzed information from "Crossroads" and other sources on all fish in the Pacific Coast states, not just salmon. His findings did not get as much attention as "Crossroads" but were even more disturbing.

Chris Frissell is an aquatic ecologist and research assistant professor at the University of Montana's Flathead Lake Biological Station. He mapped the patterns of fish decline while at Oregon State University. Chris analyzed regional patterns in the decline and extinction of all fish species in Washington, Oregon, California, and also Idaho, most of which is in the Columbia River basin. The four states included broadly ranging species with many individual stocks, such as the salmon, and species endemic to smaller areas, such as some chub species, often found in only one watershed or even just one lake. He incorporated all the information he could find on extinct species or stocks, apparently imminent extinctions, and long-term declines. He mapped his results, indicating the severity of an area's loss by darkening shades of gray. Areas with the worst levels of extinction and endangerment showed up as black clouds.

The map showed a general trend of growing endangerment from south to north, complicated by a few contrasting patches. California had 48 percent of its fish species extinct or at risk—almost half. Oregon had 33 percent of its fish species extinct or at risk, less than California, but still one-third of its fish. Washington had 13.5 percent of its fish species extinct or at risk, about one-seventh.

California had clouds of high endangerment around San Francisco Bay, which includes the Sacramento and San Joaquin River basins. Other black clouds of high endangerment were the upper Klamath Basin in Oregon, coastal streams in the Klamath Mountains, and lower Columbia River tributaries. At least six to eight species of fish were extinct or at risk in these areas.

Map, opposite: *Fish decline and extinction is not limited to a few salmon stocks. For this map, the criteria used for endangered or threatened fish were similar to criteria used in the Endangered Species Act. However, not all species classified in this study are actually listed by federal agencies as endangered or threatened. San Francisco Bay and the mainstem of the Columbia River below Grand Coulee were not mapped, since marine species and introduced fish species now play major roles in these bodies of water.*

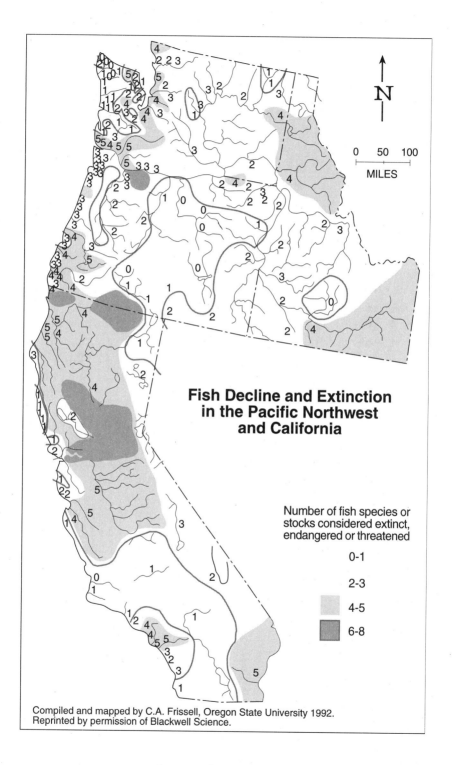

**Fish Decline and Extinction
in the Pacific Northwest
and California**

Number of fish species or
stocks considered extinct,
endangered or threatened

0-1

2-3

4-5

6-8

Compiled and mapped by C.A. Frissell, Oregon State University 1992.
Reprinted by permission of Blackwell Science.

Gray clouds, where four to five species were extinct or at risk, appeared in large areas of California, the upper Snake River basin in Idaho, the Clearwater and Spokane River basins in northern Idaho, coastal streams in southern Oregon, and the rivers of southern Puget Sound.

No single reason explained all of the clouds of endangerment. Extinctions were particularly high in watersheds with large dams, irrigation diversions, and urban development, such as the San Francisco Bay and Los Angeles areas. The Los Angeles River has been turned into a joke. Its run of winter steelhead is long extinct, and the river is famous for its large, usually dry, concrete channel across the city. The upper Klamath Basin was also affected by dams, widespread irrigation, and intensive agriculture.

But dark clouds also appeared around the lower Columbia tributaries below the dams, and along coastal streams in the Klamath Mountains, an area with no dams or large cities and little agriculture. Less severe endangerment covered much of the area between the dark clouds and included other watersheds without dams and diversions. Populations that had not been heavily fished in recent decades, such as chum salmon, were dropping. Although the study did not try to determine causes, fish decline was so widespread that it appeared multiple causes must be at work. Extensive habitat loss or degradation seemed the most likely unifying explanation.

Not all fish were dwindling. The map showed large areas where only one species or none at all were at risk. The low-risk basins were a few coastal drainages in southern and central California, the western Willamette Valley and interior desert basins of Oregon, most of the Olympic Peninsula and parts of the North Cascades in Washington, and the Wood River basin in central Idaho. Some of these basins were high-elevation watersheds that had been little disturbed by people, or arid watersheds that had fewer species of fish to begin with, or low-elevation watersheds that had escaped intensive development.

Chris found the clouds of endangerment were influenced more by the status of salmon stocks than by resident species such as suckers, chubs, and minnows. Before "Crossroads" and Chris's map, salmon were thought to be safe. They were so widespread, the reasoning went, that even if a few stocks disappeared, the species would always survive. It was now clear that salmon were declining over wide parts of their range, and their safety looked precarious. Once salmon stocks were lost from a watershed, attempts to restore them had almost always failed. Despite the expensive salmon restoration programs around the region, there were very few cases of wild salmon runs returning to their original numbers and vigor once they had declined. Where salmon had rebounded, the greatest success seemed to result from people removing obstacles in the salmon's way, backing off, and letting salmon restore themselves. Restoration was still very much in the experimental stage.

Salmon and steelhead have disappeared from wide parts of their historic ranges in the Pacific Coast states. Winter steelhead have disappeared from 25 percent of their historic range on the Pacific Coast. Summer steelhead have disappeared from 35 percent of their range, and most remaining stocks are considered to be at risk. Sea-run cutthroat trout have lost only 5 percent of their range in the region's coastal rivers, but are considered at risk in almost all of their range.

Coho salmon have disappeared from 46 percent of their original range. They are extinct in the entire eastern half of their range, which includes most rivers in the interior of the Columbia River basin, and they are seriously declining in the coastal rivers of California and Oregon. Coho are relatively secure only in Washington coastal rivers.

Chum salmon once ranged as far south as the Sacramento Basin in California. They have disappeared from rivers in California, southern Oregon, and the upper Columbia Basin, 37 percent of their original range. They are at risk in nearly half of their remaining range in Oregon and Washington.

Sockeye salmon never ranged as far south as some salmon species. They use lakes for either spawning or rearing, so only migrate up river systems that give them access to lakes. Despite their specialized life history, sockeye were once abundant in the Pacific Northwest, particularly in the Columbia River basin. But they have now disappeared from 49 percent of their original range.

Spring chinook have disappeared from 45 percent of their original range in the Pacific Coast states. Fall chinook spend less time in freshwater than most salmon and may have been less affected by degradation of freshwater habitats. They have disappeared from only 17.5 percent of their range.

"The good news is, we have done a good job of meeting most of our goals. The bad news is, we had the wrong goals," Jim Martin explained to the group of foresters in Eugene. "We tried to manage fish like they were a corn crop." Throughout the Pacific Coast states, fish management agencies had tried to maintain salmon populations through hatchery production, but they had failed to solve the biological problems causing fish to decline. Hatchery fish masked the problems for a while, but did not solve them.

Jim Lichatowich told me, "Fish culture's whole thrust was to replace rivers—we didn't try to fix habitat in rivers." The fish management agencies had a narrow focus: make more baby salmon. Then they put the fish into a landscape that no longer had enough food for salmon. They ignored the bigger problem.

The shrinking landscape of salmon means that the genetic range of each species is shrinking too. As stocks disappear, the salmon lose life history variations and local adaptations. When ranges are fragmented into isolated refugia separated by watersheds where salmon can no longer survive, the fish are unable to recolonize rivers if disturbance or disease wipes out an isolated population. The risk of total collapse becomes much greater for the species.

Firefighters learn to take the heat out of a fire by directing a hose at the base of the hottest flame. Once the heat is knocked out of the burning core, the scattered embers burn out one by one. By the mid-1990s, salmon were becoming badly scattered by Western civilization.

The salmon crisis got people's attention. Snails and clams were hardly noticed, but they were disappearing too. Five snail species from the middle Snake River were added to the federal endangered species list in recent years. The snails require well-oxygenated, cold, clean, flowing water. They are intolerant of slack water and water polluted with large quantities of dissolved herbicides, pesticides, nitrates, and phosphates, the runoff of intensive agriculture. Other snails that used to be widespread in the Columbia and Snake Rivers were reduced to tiny portions of their former ranges, and some hadn't been found in years by the few malacologists who had bothered to look.

The California floater and Willamette floater, both freshwater clams, used to be found in the lower Willamette and Columbia Rivers. In recent searches, the California floater was found only in the Okanogan River and Curlew Lake in Washington; the Willamette floater, ironically, was found only in the Fall River in California. The western pearlshell clam used to literally pave streambeds in some salmon and trout streams. But the clam's larval stage lives on the gills of the fish for a period of time before it drops to the stream bottom and forms its shell. Without the fish, the clams are slowly disappearing.

The vanishing snails and clams are indicators of how badly water quality is deteriorating in some rivers. The mollusks are also important links in aquatic food webs. Snails graze algae, and clams are filter feeders that clean the water as they strain out diatoms, bacteria, and fine organic debris. The snails and clams are—or were—a major food source for a wide range of wildlife, including trout, salmon, whitefish, sturgeon, sculpins, ducks, geese, herons, and raccoons.

When many species are declining, it's a sign of an ecosystem near collapse. It is not just a few salmon or snails that are at risk of extinction, but entire river ecosystems. The salmon crisis is just one part of a stream health crisis, and the stream health crisis is part of a watershed health crisis.

By 1997, it was naive for people to point their fingers at the dams or the clear-cuts or the cattle or the cities or the paper mills. It was everything we had done; it was all of us. We needed to point our fingers at ourselves.

INTEGRITY

Every year in September I like to find places along the McKenzie River where I can watch the wild chinook spawning. Usually I go first to the spawning channel below Trail Bridge Dam because it's one of the easiest places to see the salmon. Trail Bridge Dam blocks their access to the last couple of miles of the upper McKenzie River. As mitigation, the Eugene Water and Electric Board, which owns the dam, built a spawning channel below the dam. The artificial watercourse has perfect spawning gravels, and a gently riffling current of cold river water runs through it.

On the short walk to the channel, I try to imagine what the watery landscape must look like to the salmon. On their return from the ocean they found their way into the Columbia River, past the huge breakers on the sandbars at the river mouth. They swam upriver past the ocean freighters carrying eastern Washington wheat, past the pulp and paper mills until they detected the water of the Willamette River. As they turned into the Willamette, they passed Kelley Point Park with its sign in six languages warning people not to eat too much of the fish. They came through Portland harbor and past the restaurants, condominiums, and marinas. Then they swam upriver past more paper mills, up Willamette Falls, past the turf farms and hops fields of the valley, and then journeyed up the McKenzie. They climbed the fish ladder at Leaburg Dam and finally entered the upper McKenzie River. For their last thirty miles, they swam up a river dimpled with pools, studded with boulders, turbulent with hydraulic swirls, and cobbled with rounded river stones.

I used to see thirty or more salmon just in the spawning channel. Hundreds more were spawning in other places in the McKenzie watershed.

This year I see four salmon. Their behavior tells me I am seeing one female and three males. One salmon swims up and down the channel, and another follows her closely, never more than a foot or two behind. The other two follow at a distance. Occasionally one tries to approach the female, and the first male chases it away. Two of the males have lines of white fungus along their backs. They're dying; they'll need to spawn soon.

The water in the river is cold and clean. The water is clean in many of the rivers all over the Pacific Northwest where salmon populations are crashing. But can I call this river, with its engineered spawning channel and four salmon, healthy?

The federal Clean Water Act was passed in 1972. Its goal is "to restore and maintain the chemical, physical, and biological integrity of the Nation's waters." Chemical integrity could be measured by analyzing water samples, and numerical standards could be set. How could biological integrity be measured? *Integrity* suggests wholeness, completeness, health.

Jim Karr is a professor of fisheries and zoology at the University of Washington. He has researched, written, and spoken widely on stream ecology and biological integrity in streams. He was educated as an ornithologist, not as a fish biologist, a background that he sees as an advantage. "As an outsider," he tells me, "I asked questions that people trained to look at fish didn't ask. People trained outside an area can look at the problem in a different way."

Jim started working with streams and fish in the Midwest in the early 1970s, as part of a project funded by the Environmental Protection Agency (EPA). The EPA officials were implementing the new Clean Water Act as if crystal-clear water were the only goal. Cleaning up chemicals and sewage was certainly an improvement in water quality, but Jim saw that it wasn't enough to make rivers healthy. The river ecosystems still did not recover after chemicals stopped pouring into the water.

Jim pointed out to the officials that their approach was not fixing the problem. One man told him, "We don't care if it's making the river better—we care if it's implementing the Clean Water Act." They were restoring the chemical integrity of rivers but were not yet paying attention to the law's requirement to restore biological integrity.

In the years since his Midwest experience, Jim has given a lot of time to the problem of defining and measuring biological integrity. Biological integrity means that a river has the complete community of native organisms that a comparable, pristine river in the region would have. The river also needs to have the full range of biological processes—the basic processes of ecosystems, such as energy production (food source), reproduction, competition, and predation; and the long-term processes of adaptation. The river must have a diverse, thriving community of living plants and animals, and it also has to be dynamic and resilient.

People's activities change and degrade rivers by altering the food or energy sources, the water quality, the habitat structure, the flow regime, and the biotic interactions of the river ecosystems. Chemical criteria only measure water quality, and since they don't measure sediment or temperature, they are only a partial measure of water quality. A channelized, lifeless river could meet Clean Water Act standards as long as its water was free of chemical contaminants. The law didn't require that water be left in rivers—a dry river could meet the criteria.

Clean rivers were an improvement. But Jim Karr believes that the goal should be healthy rivers, not just chemical-free rivers. To be healthy, rivers

To understand our rivers today, we must know their history (log drive, McKenzie River, circa 1910). (photo courtesy Lane County Historical Museum, L4C/L71-318)

have to have biological integrity. Jim developed the Index of Biotic Integrity (IBI) as a scientifically sound, yet fairly simple and cost-effective, way to measure integrity.

The index is similar to a battery of medical tests for a person: blood pressure, urinalysis, white-blood-cell count, cholesterol level, and so forth. Good health is more than just good test results, but the tests do measure a lot of key indicators of health. The index was designed to be a supplement to chemical analysis, not a replacement.

Jim based his index on a river's fish community. Integrity could not be judged by salmon alone because they were affected by events outside the watershed, but salmon would be included as the river's entire fish community was evaluated. Biologists needed to tailor the index for the river ecosystems in their region, but the general principles worked for all rivers.

The index requires a sample of all fish in a river. They reveal the full range of ecological effects at work in the river, but only when the structure of the fish community is assessed, as well as the abundance of fish and the condition of individual fish.

The index begins by counting the total number of native fish species. It also looks at the structure of the fish community—that is, how many species of different groups are present: bottom-dwelling species, such as dace and sculpins; water column species, with trout as one example; long-lived species such as suckers and sturgeon; species intolerant of pollution and human disturbance; and species tolerant of pollution, which are more common in degraded streams.

The evaluation then looks at the fish community from another angle. The index counts how many species are omnivores that will eat anything, how many eat insects and other invertebrates, and how many eat other fish. The piscivores, or fish-eating fish, are the top carnivores in the stream. Degraded streams have a greater percentage of omnivores, and the proportion of insect-eating fish and piscivores decreases.

Finally, the index looks at the abundance of fish in the stream, and the percentage of fish that have diseases, tumors, fin damage, or skeletal deformities. These sorts of problems increase in degraded areas, especially rivers with toxic contaminants.

Degraded rivers are dominated by fish that eat anything, tolerate high levels of pollution, and are habitat generalists. Few top carnivores like bull trout are present. Growth rates are low and fish condition is poor. Hybrids—crosses between native fish and introduced fish species—are found. Diseased and deformed fish are present, or are even common.

The state of a river's health is revealed by its humblest creatures. Stonefly nymphs, which emerged as adults here, survive only in high quality water. (Val Rapp)

Rivers with high levels of biotic integrity are healthy rivers. Their good health shows in their fish communities. They have the complete range of native fish for their region, and they have fish of all ages, just as a healthy human community has all ages, from babies to old people. Healthy rivers have fish that are intolerant of pollution and predatory fish at the top of the food chain. Individual fish are in good condition. Diseased and deformed fish are rare.

Jim Karr developed the original Index of Biotic Integrity to use with fish, but he has also developed versions to use with aquatic insect larvae—the mayfly, caddisfly, stonefly, and other larvae in streams. "Stream insects are probably even better than fish," he told me. The insect species have well-defined tolerances for pollution, and the presence or absence of particular species is an important sign of a river's water quality. Some species tolerate pollution, and others live only in cold, well-oxygenated, pure water. Like fish, the insect community has a complex structure. The insect community may have even more variety than the fish community.

The proportion of grazers, scrapers, predators, and so on in the insect community is a valuable clue to the river's condition.

The Index of Biotic Integrity is an addition to chemical criteria, not a substitute for them. It is a quick, reliable, cost-effective way to measure the effects of all human impacts on the river ecosystem. The index also detects any type of degradation, not just chemical pollution. It shows the effects of dams, channelizing, sediment, and changed river flows. The index also shows the effects of activities that might not be apparent at the time the river is tested, such as water withdrawals that happen only in certain seasons, or flushes of sediment that occur only in rainstorms.

But in the end, the index is just a tool. The data must be translated into statements about the ecological health of the river. Once we know the river's state of health, we need to respond.

The beauty of biological integrity in rivers is that it also expresses biological integrity in watersheds. Jim Karr said, "Rivers are the circulatory system of landscape. Ultimately, they are the integrators of watersheds and also of our actions."

I first got interested in river health because I loved the Pacific Northwest's beautiful rivers and wild salmon. Now I understand that the best way to measure river health is by the humblest creatures in our rivers—the stoneflies and the suckers. If the insects can't live, if the suckers have no eyes, if the otters have no testicles, the rivers are not healthy. No matter how beautiful they are.

Chapter 9

Restoration

W hile the lightning fires were burning in the John Day Basin in August 1996 and Gene and I were hiking up the North Fork, the Forest Service was working on a restoration project in the North Fork's floodplain. On our way in, we saw the heavy equipment tearing apart rock piles left by the dredge mining. At the end of our hike, back at our truck, we talked to the Forest Service engineer in charge of the work, Ed Calame.

Ed told us how his approach to river restoration had changed over the years. He used to do projects like dumping truckloads of spawning-size gravel into the North Fork's tributary streams. The fish used the new gravels, but Ed eventually realized that the small number of salmon in the watershed already had more spawning areas than they could use. Lack of gravel was not the limiting factor. The salmon needed a healthy, functioning river along the entire length, not just for the few miles of upper river inside the wilderness boundary.

"The river can take care of itself a lot better than we ever can," Ed told Gene and me. "All we have to do is unlock it."

The river would heal itself—renew the spawning gravels, provide plenty of food for young salmon and trout, offer cool water in deep pools in late summer—if we gave it a chance. The long rows of armored dredge piles locked up the floodplain.

The heavy equipment was breaking up the dredge piles. The operators put large boulders down first, then finer gravels on top as they flattened the stacks and re-created a floodplain. They saved as many trees and clumps of riparian shrubs as possible during the work and would later reseed the restored floodplain with native seed.

Now, in late August, the restored floodplain looked like a dry, dusty

The river has been unable to break down these dredge piles in fifty years (North Fork John Day). A Forest Service project will restore the floodplain and give the river the chance to heal itself. (Val Rapp)

gravel plain. But the river would complete the restoration project over the next several years. Floods would sculpt the floodplain into side channels, gravel bars, complex edges, and riparian habitats. Driftwood logs would create new logjams, which in turn would create additional habitats. The floodplain would absorb water while floods covered it and release the water to the river during summer low flows. The subsurface water would be cool and keep river temperatures down. Cottonwoods, alders, creek dogwoods, and elderberries would shade the braided channels and provide shelter and food to birds, beavers, and other animals.

"When a floodplain's working right, everybody benefits," Ed told us.

BASIC PRINCIPLES
We haven't really tried stream restoration yet in the Pacific Northwest. We tried to replace rivers with hatcheries and to engineer rivers with techno-fixes instead of helping them to heal themselves.

We are beginners at the art and science of river restoration. Science and history are helping us understand healthy rivers and how we have changed our rivers. Some basic principles are starting to emerge from our new understanding, but we need to approach restoration work with humility. We will learn much more.

Work with the natural strengths of the ecosystem. Avoid techno-fixes. Restoration projects must be designed to work with the strengths of river ecosystems: connectivity, complexity, dynamic equilibrium, and the stock structure of salmon and trout species. Hatcheries often treated salmon stocks like interchangeable widgets, freely transplanting them from basin to basin. Restoration work was often planned with little understanding of rivers' dynamic processes.

The North Fork floodplain project works with the river's natural strengths. Other undertakings in the John Day Basin do not. One project tried to restore river structure by building low rock wing dams at intervals along the shore. The periodic partial barriers were designed to help the river hold sediment and rebuild its eroded edges. But the scheme ignored the river's connections to the watershed. Cattle were still allowed free access to the river, and the riparian area and banks continued to be trampled and bare. The dams further disrupted the river's already damaged interactions with its floodplain. A project in a tributary stream installed log weirs so the stream would scour pools below each weir. The number of pools did increase slightly but did nothing for the stream's biggest problem, high water temperature. The solution of the temperature problem would require looking at the stream's connections to its riparian area, floodplain, and watershed.

Restore health. Don't apply Band-Aids to a patient in cardiac arrest. Consider this medical emergency: A patient is brought to the hospital in cardiac arrest, with a deep cut on one arm and a broken leg. If the doctor bandages the wound and sets the broken leg first, the patient will die. The cardiac arrest needs to be dealt with right away if the patient's life is to be saved.

Traditional approaches to stream restoration have usually been Band-Aids on patients in cardiac arrest. One of the most common activities is putting logs in streams. The logs are often set down in carefully designed arrangements and cabled in place. These projects are satisfying to us in many ways. We feel that the river has been fixed—we can point to the repairs. The work can be finished quickly, and it can be done without making any real changes in the way we treat streams and watersheds. But instream structure projects are usually the worst way to spend

Fish racks on the McKenzie River blocked the migration of wild salmon to home streams (circa 1920). The salmon were used to produce hatchery stock. (photo courtesy Lane County Historical Museum, M1A/L78-246/98. Smith Mountjoy Collection)

scarce restoration money. The greater ecological need is to restore the watershed's ability to supply the stream with large fallen trees.

The same principle is true for all river restoration. We have disabled rivers that used to be self-sustaining, self-healing ecosystems. We should restore rivers to health so they can function normally again, not manage them to compensate for the degradation we've caused. We should rebuild rivers so they can once again supply food and habitat for young salmon and trout, not build more hatcheries to produce baby fish.

Manage people, not rivers or salmon. Rivers can heal themselves if we give them the chance. Over and over again, I heard the message that we need to manage ourselves, not rivers. We need to manage the impacts that we have on rivers, floodplains, and watersheds. University of Washington professor Jim Karr told me:

> *We manage the people, not the land. There's a level of hubris—that we manage salmon. Northwest river systems have been making salmon for millennia. We need to manage people so natural systems can make salmon as they've done for a long time. When we manage salmon, we barge fish, rely too much on hatcheries, and so forth.*

Fisheries consultant Jim Lichatowich took this idea a step further. "Salmon would be fools to hire us as managers," he said bluntly. "If the salmon depend on hatcheries, they ultimately depend on politicians. This is not a very good place to be in."

For a hundred years, fish management agencies promoted hatcheries heavily as the answer to declining salmon runs. But hatcheries are an economic problem as well as a biological one. Hatcheries are just as vulnerable to budget cuts as any other government program. Salmon fry have been released prematurely from hatcheries because of budget shortfalls, and some hatcheries may be forced to close as budgets continue to get tighter.

Since hatchery fish were already a problem, is this really a disaster? Jim Lichatowich explained:

The nature of the disaster is like a person who smokes heavily for many years and eventually is on a respirator, and then a power failure occurs. The power failure is a disaster for that person, but smoking for all those years was the bigger disaster. So the premature release of salmon from the hatcheries was a disaster, but the bigger disaster is that we allowed the situation to get to where the salmon depend so much on the hatcheries.

When rivers are healthy, salmon will manage themselves without any tax dollars at all. If we manage our cities, farms, and forests so rivers can be healthy, then rivers won't need our money or management to make them work.

PRINCIPLES FOR A PLAN OF ACTION

The three basic concepts discussed above underlie all the principles for a restoration plan.

Save the last best places first. Traditional restoration focused on finding the degraded areas and fixing them. This approach assumed that there were only a few degraded spots, surrounded by a healthy landscape. But in fact, healthy watersheds are isolated refugia in the radically changed environment of the Pacific Northwest. In the 1980s, biologists recognized that we need to protect the remaining healthy rivers first—a reversal of the old approach. The last best places are the strongholds for many threatened and endangered species. Biologist Chris Frissell warned, "Once a watershed is broken, we really don't know how to fix it."

This principle is slowly being put into practice. The Forest Service and Bureau of Land Management have begun to identify key, or core, watersheds on the public lands they manage. Outside government, The Nature Conservancy has campaigned to save the last best places in each state as refuges. Pacific Rivers Council has worked to educate people about this idea and other restoration principles through workshops, publications, and input to government agencies.

Protect healthy rivers. Prevent damage: unload loaded guns. Healthy watersheds and rivers are not protected simply by being designated as key watersheds or reserves or wild and scenic rivers. Once protected, they must be secured. The loaded guns in the watershed must be very carefully unloaded—old logging roads rehabilitated or removed before they slide, failing culverts replaced, cut banks stabilized, cattle excluded from streams and riparian areas, tailing piles from old mines stabilized or removed, and so forth.

The greatest danger for healthy watersheds is people. We need to manage ourselves so that we do not destroy rivers we love.

Do no harm. Be careful not to create additional damage. In the 1970s, fish biologists promoted stream cleaning. Loggers were required to remove wood from streams after they had finished logging an area. Crews were hired to clear major logjams from streams and rivers. It was routine to remove logs from rivers after floods. Stream cleaning sounds like it should be good for the streams, and fish biologists told us that it was. They had the idea that a clean stream was a good stream. They thought that large logjams blocked migrating fish, and that too much wood in rivers would use up all the dissolved oxygen in the water as the wood decayed. One of my first jobs in forestry was to clean wood out of streams.

About the time that stream cleaning was reaching its peak in the late 1970s, ecologists were beginning to understand how important wood was for healthy rivers. Getting government agencies to change their direction is like turning an ocean liner—it takes time. But once agencies make the turn, they follow the new direction enthusiastically. Hundreds of projects sprouted to put logs back in streams.

But many of these well-intentioned endeavors have had what biologists dryly call "unintended negative effects." Poorly placed logs have caused streams to downcut, further isolating them from their floodplains, or have resulted in destabilized stream banks. At their best, projects to put logs into streams are usually not the most cost-effective restoration. The floods of 1996 put more trees into the rivers and streams, for free, than years of restoration work could have accomplished. Unfortunately, in some places, landowners were busy pulling wood out after the flood while at the same time more projects were being planned to put wood into streams in the upper parts of the same watersheds.

One Forest Service engineer told me he figured that in his career so far he had, by poorly designed culverts, blocked fish passage in fifteen streams. He liked to fish and had no intention of damaging the runs. "I just didn't think about it in those days," he said. Now he was designing corrective projects that replaced the older culverts. With a few more years until retirement, he thought he might work long enough to restore the fish passage in fifteen streams, balancing out the damage he had unintentionally done earlier.

Of course, tax dollars paid for most of the stream cleaning in the 1970s, and paid for projects to put wood back in streams in the 1990s. Tax money paid for culverts that blocked fish, and again for the culvert replacements.

Work on a watershed basis. The creation of nature preserves is a land-based idea that is meaningless for rivers. Most river protection campaigns are focused on the upper parts of watersheds. Lower rivers were degraded so early that most people do not realize they were once the most productive parts of the rivers.

River habitats have to be continuously connected like links in a long chain. Most rivers have many broken links. Broken links are like pulled stitches in a sweater—when one stitch is broken, it leads to the others unraveling. Restoration projects are often useless if they focus on one small spot and ignore the watershed context. Remember the old saying, "Think globally, act locally." With rivers, we need to think about the whole watershed before we act locally.

Develop individual prescriptions for each watershed. Doctors need to know science, but they practice medicine, which is different. Scientists lump individuals into groups and look for general principles. A doctor separates the individual from the group in order to understand the patient's unique constellation of conditions. Then the doctor makes a diagnosis and develops a treatment plan, or a prescription, that addresses that diagnosis. Jim Karr commented:

> *The prescriptions we hear are often general: remove dams. But that's like a doctor treating a patient with a prescription based on the average patient he sees, instead of making an individual diagnosis. We need to diagnose the symptoms in each patient, instead of trying to use a general prescription.*

Each watershed has an individual history. Each river basin has a character formed by a unique combination of geology, climate, biology, and human history. Salmon know their own river by the smell of its water. They have adapted their life histories to the unique character of their own watershed. Knowing our watersheds will take time.

Connect healthy areas to each other. We have ideas about how to restore high-quality habitat, but we don't know for sure how to do it. All restoration is experimental at this point, and so we should be conservative in our approaches. After protecting the last best places, the next priority is to connect healthy areas to each other. We need to build toward fully connected, self-sustaining ecosystems.

Often reconnection comes in the form of restoring fish passage to high-quality habitat. In the McKenzie watershed, a poorly designed culvert blocked bull trout access to a prime spawning stream when the highway was built in 1959. Forest Service biologists, in partnership with other agencies, replaced the Olallie Creek culvert in 1995. Bull trout were seen using the new culvert less than one month later, and nine redds (gravel "nests" in streams) were counted in the newly connected stream reach in the first spawning season.

Reconnecting streams is the best ecological approach, and the most cost-effective as well. One comparison of various projects found that putting logs in streams typically resulted in only a few dozen more salmon smolts produced for each action completed. Fish passage projects generated thousands of salmon smolts per project. The instream wood placements were a lot cheaper than the fish passage corrections, but smolt production was so low that the cost per smolt was $13.93. The more expensive, but far more effective, fish passage work cost only $0.30 per smolt.

The removal of the two Elwha River dams on the northern Olympic Peninsula may be the single most important restoration project in the Pacific Northwest. As the site of the largest dam demolition project ever attempted in the region, the Elwha would be a living laboratory where we could learn how a river restores itself from the ecological disaster of dams. The biggest challenge would be dealing with the accumulated sediments in the two reservoirs. If the proposal is funded, the National Park Service plans to tear down the dams in steps and let the sediments flush downriver in pulses that would not inundate the private property below.

The Elwha dam removal has the potential to be the most cost-effective restoration project in the region as well. Chris Frissell has evaluated the potential of various restoration options in the northern Olympic Peninsula.

Projects that reconnect pristine habitat are often more cost-effective than attempts to restore degraded habitat. Bull trout uses new culvert to reach spawning stream. (photo courtesy USDA Forest Service, Jim Capurso photo)

Once the Elwha is reconnected, it will need no other restoration work. Most of the Elwha watershed is pristine habitat, and it is protected in Olympic National Park. Nearby rivers are far more degraded and would require long-term, expensive restoration work, much of it experimental. "Dam removal on the Elwha would give the biggest bang for the buck for salmon restoration in that area," Chris told me. "It would be better to remove the dams on the Elwha and allow salmon access to the existing high-quality habitat, than try to restore the habitat in the other rivers."

Unlock rivers so they can function normally. Jim Lichatowich commented:

> *Rivers and salmon can heal themselves if we manage our activities so that they have that chance. A lot of healing rivers is still a natural process. Rivers know how to do that, and salmon know how to do that, but we don't know how. It's presumptuous to think that we do. We need to clear obstacles to rivers healing and let them do it.*

But we do need to remove obstacles. After rivers have been degraded, they may stay in their unhealthy condition for decades with little natural recovery. The North Fork of the John Day River was unable to break down dredge mining piles in fifty years. In eastern Oregon and Washington, grazing was reduced sharply after World War I, but stream surveys in the 1980s found that rivers had not recovered very much. Charley Dewberry, the Pacific Rivers Council stream restoration coordinator, learned that the Siuslaw River in Oregon had cut down to bedrock by the late 1800s after its large logjams were removed. The river stayed that way for a hundred years.

We don't know how long it would take degraded streams to recover. After the last ice age, it took five thousand to eight thousand years for the Pacific Northwest rivers to explode with salmon populations. It took that long for the mountains and rivers to create the forests, stream habitats, and food webs that made abundant salmon populations possible. We are an impatient people; five years seems like a long time to us. Most of us are probably not willing to wait five thousand years for rivers to recover on their own.

Restore watershed functions and processes. Ecosystems work by themselves when they're healthy. They don't need to be managed or enhanced.

On the Middle Fork of the John Day River, The Nature Conservancy preserve manager Ramon Lara and his staff are restoring the river so it can function the way it did before. They have fenced out cattle, are letting trees and shrubs return to the riparian area, and are opening up old river meanders and side channels that were closed off. They are managing the site by taking away the legacies of past management.

A properly functioning, self-sustaining river benefits us too. There's almost no end to the work that rivers will do for us if we give them a chance. Riparian forests clean nonpoint pollution from the water and keep it out of rivers. A healthy riparian forest could save possibly millions of dollars in water treatment costs. Floodplains and wetlands absorb floods and purify water, preventing millions of dollars in flood damage. The purchase of conservation easements on these areas is far less expensive than the construction of dams and levees, and no maintenance is necessary. If salmon came back in the numbers that they did in the late 1800s, they would be a major food source, and one produced without the use of farmland, fertilizer, or pesticides; and the fishery would support thousands of jobs, just as it did before.

Expect disturbance. Plan for resilience in the face of change. You do not rebuild healthy rivers by eliminating change. Oregon State University professor Stan Gregory remarked:

If restoration doesn't understand and allow disturbance, we try to preserve a stability that isn't natural. But we need a large enough area to absorb the full range of disturbance. If only a small watershed is pristine, and it is affected by a flood . . . He shrugged.

We need to plan for floods and other disturbances when we restore rivers, instead of constructing projects that look great on a summer day when the river is low and calm.

Reconnect people to rivers and watersheds. Involve your community. It takes a community to create a healthy watershed. Jim Karr pointed out:

The local watershed groups are tremendously important. The group makes a connection between a place and the things people cherish in that place—it invests them with a sense of responsibility in their regional environment.

People from the community can diagnose their river and watershed instead of receiving a top-down prescription. When local communities get passionate about the condition of their river and their salmon, they do something.

We know our landscape by the lines of roads and the web of our developments. The change to watershed thinking is tough. Many government groups, private landowners, and community organizations all want—and need—to be involved. Before the Forest Service could start its floodplain restoration project on the North Fork of the John Day, it had to get permits or approvals from seventeen different agencies. The McKenzie Watershed Council has twenty members, representing government agencies, key interests, and stakeholders in the watershed. Progress can be excruciatingly slow.

But the more established watershed councils are succeeding in carrying out some restoration work that is rebuilding ecological processes, improving water quality, and allowing salmon runs to recover. The Coquille River watershed in southern Oregon, the Chehalis River watershed in western Washington, and the McKenzie River watershed in the Oregon Cascades are just three examples of river basins where watershed groups are beginning to get results. Some landowners fear intrusions on their property rights. But a watershed approach is based on cooperation, not control or appropriation. It's founded on a shared

At Three Mile Dam on the Umatilla River, restoration includes fish passage for smolts and adults, but irrigation dewaters the river. (Gene Skrine)

sense of responsibility and respect, a mutual understanding of our need for sustenance.

The state and federal governments still have important roles beyond the watershed council level. Bad management by one community affects many other communities downstream. Jim Karr commented:

> *If people don't have a sense of place, other people should be able to regulate their bad behavior. That can come in the form of regulations or incentives.*

Use diverse strategies. Protect diversity in your watershed. To restore salmon, we have to think like salmon. The salmon have developed hundreds of life history variations and local adaptations in order to deal with changing conditions and as hedges against natural disturbances. Oregon coho restoration team leader Jim Martin remarked:

> *We don't know the perfect strategy, so we need to have a lot of strategies. We need a lot of diverse strategies in different watersheds. And we need to monitor closely so we don't follow our mistakes for very long.*

Give rivers some space. Protect floodplains and riparian areas from people. Jim Karr noted:

We should protect floodplains from humans more than we protect humans from floodplains. We should not let people go back in and live on floodplains again. If people take that risk again, we shouldn't pay to fix it for them. We should require people to build out of floodplains rather than sell flood insurance.

The River Network, a nonprofit organization, had already started the Willamette Floodplain Restoration Project when the big flood rolled through the valley in February 1996. The flood helped to create a teachable moment, a moment when people were willing to consider new ways of doing things. The project's goal is to restore fifty thousand acres of the historic Willamette River floodplain. River Network is joining with the Army Corps of Engineers, the Oregon Department of Fish and Wildlife, and other agencies, cities, and organizations throughout the Willamette Valley to identify restoration sites where the river would be allowed to have its natural floodplain, wetlands, and side channels. Their engineering consultants, Philip Williams & Associates, Ltd., estimated that fifty thousand acres of natural valley storage could reduce the peak flows of a major flood by up to 18 percent.

The floodplain restoration approach could work for other lowland rivers that originally had extensive floodplains, such as rivers that flow into Puget Sound. Levees protect property next to the embankments but create an even greater hazard downstream as they funnel all the floodwater down the river channel instead of letting it disperse on floodplains. Natural floodplains could reduce peak flows and protect property downstream.

Some land uses would be compatible with floodplains. The James River Corporation and other companies are experimenting with farms of hybrid cottonwoods, where flood-tolerant trees are planted in low-lying areas along rivers. The trees are harvested only once every seven years, less often than most other farm crops. Wood fiber from the cottonwoods is used for pulp and paper and could help take logging pressure off forests on steep slopes in the future. Other low-intensity agricultural uses might also be compatible with floodplains.

The Willamette greenway ended up as a less ambitious system of parks and boat landings. First conceived in the 1960s, the original idea was ahead of its time but may be reborn yet. We have established the concept of protected riparian zones in forestry. Loggers are now required to leave trees along stream banks and in a strip along the watercourse. Specific requirements vary in different states, and also depend on the stream size, with larger, fish-bearing streams getting wider buffers.

The riparian forest is the heart of a healthy, resilient river. We need to protect riparian zones through land in agricultural, residential, and urban areas, as well as forests. Riparian buffers would be designed differently in these populated regions than in forests. Over the decades, healthy green corridors of water and trees would connect the entire landscape. Yet the simple idea of fencing cattle out of streams, and supplying them with water tanks and shade away from streams, is still hotly contested.

In rivers with dams, mimic pre-dam flow patterns as much as possible, in balance with other needs. We're not going to take out most of the dams. We depend on the big dams for flood control, power, irrigation water, and navigation. In the Elwha watershed, dam removal is a good strategy because there is so much pristine habitat above the dams. In river systems like the Columbia, agriculture, grazing, and other land uses have had major impacts on the rivers. Dam removal would not produce much restoration. Expensive programs with uncertain results would be needed to restore the rivers. Adding structures or engineering habitat downstream from dams is usually ineffective.

But it may be possible, in some cases, to operate dams in ways that are closer to natural river processes. It may be possible to manage water releases that mimic natural freshets. These "managed floods" would flush fine sediments from spawning gravels, rebuild channels and floodplains, and allow flood-dependent fish to complete their life cycles. Managed floods could be another seductive techno-fix, and many unintended side effects are possible. Water releases could erode river channels instead of rebuilding. Prescriptions would have to be individual for each dam and each river.

Rivers need water. Work with the community in your watershed to establish minimum instream flows. Fish need water. They don't travel well on dirt bikes. But farmers need water too. Abandoned irrigated fields don't revert to natural vegetation. Introduced weeds like thistles quickly take over the fields, and wind blows the dry soil away. More efficient irrigation systems could reduce water needs. But many rivers are overappropriated now, and any water saved would only go to people with junior water rights, not stay in the river. Instream flow problems need to be addressed at the watershed level or the state level. Communities will have to find a balance between human needs and their responsibilities as good stewards of rivers.

Work with a long-term perspective. The return to good health will take years. Jim Lichatowich emphasized:

> *Yes, there are enough elements left for recovery to begin. It will be a long-term process, but there's enough to start. Trying to let rivers recover is a whole new approach. People don't appreciate this. They expect to see results in two to four years.*

When I asked Forest Service research scientist Gordon Reeves what improvements we would see in twenty years with our river restoration work, he predicted:

> *We'll see improvements in the areas that are not as degraded. We may see improvement in those areas with wood; they will develop structure quickly. Very degraded areas will take one hundred plus years to recover.*

Develop feedback loops. Monitor, learn, and change. Stay in touch with your watershed. A biologist for a federal agency told me he couldn't answer my questions about the juvenile salmon in the lower Columbia River as well as he would like because his agency wasn't monitoring the fish. Monitoring means keeping track of what's going on in the field, watching the results of projects, gathering data. He explained that work would get funded, but usually there was no money set aside for monitoring afterwards. Programs were called successful if they were completed as planned. But without monitoring, there was no way to tell if the work actually got the intended results. He had submitted proposals for monitoring, but he didn't get the funds. "We spend a lot of time pushing paper and talking about data," he commented, "but not much time collecting data."

We are beginners at river restoration. We need to monitor our projects to see what really happens. Jim Lichatowich commented, "We were ignorant of many of the ecological processes while we were destroying them, but we'll never be able to restore rivers with the same level of ignorance."

PRINCIPLES FOR WATERSHED RESTORATION

Basic Principles

1. Work with the natural strengths of the ecosystem. Avoid techno-fixes.
2. Restore health. Don't apply Band-Aids to a patient in cardiac arrest.
3. Manage people, not rivers or salmon. Rivers can heal themselves if we give them the chance.

Principles for a Plan of Action

1. Save the last best places first.
2. Protect healthy rivers. Prevent damage: unload loaded guns.
3. Do no harm. Be careful not to create additional damage.
4. Work on a watershed basis.
5. Develop individual prescriptions for each watershed.
6. Connect healthy areas to each other.
7. Unlock rivers so they can function normally.
8. Restore watershed functions and processes.
9. Expect disturbance. Plan for resilience in the face of change.
10. Reconnect people to rivers and watersheds. Involve your community.
11. Use diverse strategies. Protect diversity in your watershed.
12. Give rivers some space. Protect floodplains and riparian areas from people.
13. In rivers with dams, mimic pre-dam flow patterns as much as possible, in balance with other needs.
14. Rivers need water. Work with the community in your watershed to establish minimum instream flows.
15. Work with a long-term perspective. The return to good health will take years.
16. Develop feedback loops. Monitor, learn, and change. Stay in touch with your watershed.

Chapter 10

Refuge

No place on earth has a better shot at reconciling people and nature than the Pacific Northwest, the greenest corner of history's richest civilization.

—*John C. Ryan, State of the Northwest*

CONSEQUENCES

Floods have always existed. Flood damage is new. It never happened until people moved onto floodplains and into mountain canyons. As the Maginot Line of dams and levees spread across the watersheds of the Pacific Northwest in the twentieth century, people thought they were protected from floods. People forgot, or never knew, that floods and landslides are a normal part of the landscape. They thought the rivers were just another part of the postcard-pretty backdrop to their modern, high-tech cities.

The Christmas flood of 1964 in western Oregon was labeled as a hundred-year flood when it happened, and it kept that reputation in regional folk history. I'd heard about the famous Christmas flood ever since I came to Oregon in 1977. I wondered how many years I'd have to live here before I saw a big flood. When the first flood of 1996 happened in February, newspapers and TV stations called it a hundred-year flood. When some areas in western Oregon were inundated again that November, news media reported that there was a second hundred-year flood in the same year. Some reporters found it remarkable that there was a hundred-year flood in 1964 and again just thirty-two years later, and then again just six months later. No one doubted the news media, least of all themselves, and no one asked the obvious question—were these really hundred-year floods?

Instead, many people concluded that hundred-year floods were happening more often now. They didn't blame themselves for not giving rivers enough space to act like rivers—for living on floodplains, draining wetlands, and channelizing the waterways. People didn't think about whether or not they were living in a way that fit with natural systems—they blamed rivers for not fitting in with society.

Jim Lichatowich commented on the 1996 flood:

The flood is like El Niño. The things we've done cause natural events to become problems. The salmon coped with floods and El Niños for thousands of years, but they haven't coped with us. We've torn up the habitat for 150 years, and then we point to events that have been there for thousands of years, saying they're the culprit for salmon decline. If the rivers had been healthy and the stocks healthy, they could have absorbed the flood.

In fact, the floods of 1996 were not hundred-year floods except in a few of the hardest-hit areas. The flood of record for the Willamette River was in December 1861, when the river had a peak flow of 500,000 cubic feet per second (CFS). The Willamette's peak flow in 1996 was 365,000 CFS, considerably less. In the last 135 years, the Willamette had four floods that were larger than the 1996 flood—in 1861, 1881, 1890, and 1964. Several others were almost as large as the 1996 flood. For the Willamette River, the February 1996 flood was closer to a thirty-year flood than a hundred-year flood.

On the McKenzie River, the 1996 flood was the size of a typical five-year flood before the dams were built in the 1960s. The Tualatin River near Portland was rated as having a ten-year flood. Where the cells of heaviest rain parked over watersheds, a few rivers really did have hundred-year floods. The Nehalem and Wilson Rivers in northwest Oregon; the Grande Ronde, Umatilla, Metolius, and Deschutes Rivers in eastern Oregon; and the Sandy and Clackamas Rivers east of Portland were all rated as having true hundred-year floods.

The long intervals between floods make it difficult to learn from the events. People didn't know they were living on floodplains because the last flood was outside their experience. County zoning officials didn't know they were permitting construction on floodplains because most had

On February 4, 1890, floodwaters from the Willamette River surrounded the original Ferry Street Bridge in Eugene, Oregon. (photo courtesy Lane County Historical Museum, 13A7/L76-981)

started their careers after the 1964 flood. In many cases, home builders and officials thought that the new dams and levees completed since 1964 protected them. I heard about the 1964 flood because I lived in a rural area and also because I was interested in rivers. The Pacific Northwest's population was mostly urban, and city dwellers didn't hear much about the history of their landscape. In 1990, with almost 3 million people, Oregon's population was over 70 percent urban. Washington's population was more than 76 percent urban, out of almost 5 million people. Even lightly populated Idaho, with just over 1 million people, was over 57 percent urban.

Thirty-two years is about the span of an average professional career, so only a few hydrologists and fish biologists near retirement age remembered the 1964 flood as a professional experience. Some middle-aged professionals recalled the event from living through it as kids. How did the 1964 flood affect rivers and fish? How long did biological recovery take? No one knew. We had lost our opportunity to learn from the past, but there were lessons to be learned from the 1996 floods.

Portland's thriving riverfront escaped serious damage in the flood of 1996, but is vulnerable to future floods. (Gene Skrine)

The floods of 1996 had opposite effects on healthy and unhealthy rivers. The McKenzie River, a fairly healthy river, acquired hundreds of new driftwood logs and held on to most of them. The logjams in the delta area grew larger and more complex. Gravel bars were scrubbed clean and renewed. Landslides added new boulders and wood to streams, and the currents sculpted more complex channels. Some homes were damaged along the lower McKenzie River, roads were ruined, and sediment loads were high in the river for a couple of days. People suffered some losses, but the river digested the flood well.

On the other hand, in the Tillamook Basin of northwest Oregon, the Wilson and Nehalem Rivers scoured their channels and were badly scarred. Much of the Tillamook Basin had burned repeatedly in large forest fires in 1933, 1939, and 1945. After the fires, logging roads had been put in hastily and the timber salvaged. Mountainsides and rivers were bare after the burned trees were yarded out. With the timber gone, logging companies defaulted on their property taxes. The counties ended up owning thousands of acres of timberland, which they asked the Oregon Department of Forestry to manage for them. The forestry department planted trees through the 1950s, but they had inherited a tough situation. They would not be able to manage the coming flood.

By 1996, the slopes were covered with young trees. But the old, poorly built roads and culverts were prone to failures and washouts, and the landscape was naturally slide-prone anyway because of the underlying layers of sandstone. These vulnerable mountain slopes got the heaviest rains of any area in Oregon in February 1996. The Nehalem River crested at 27.4 feet, more than 13 feet above flood stage. Roughly two hundred homes were destroyed or badly damaged along the Nehalem, and houses were also ruined along the Wilson and Tillamook Rivers. Some dairy farmers lost most of their herds, in an area noted for its Tillamook cheeses.

Along the Wilson River, virtually every tributary stream gouged its channel down to bedrock. The streams looked like rock flumes shooting down mountain draws to the river. The Wilson River dug at the sides of its channel viciously. Banks were scrubbed to bare dirt for long, continuous stretches interrupted only by rock cliffs. Driftwood logs were left perched on rock outcroppings almost thirty feet above the river's normal level. Most logs were carried out of the system. The Nehalem River also chiseled its channel for long distances. Whole lines of alders toppled along its banks. In a way, the flood scars were one more legacy from the earlier forest fires. The rivers were left badly damaged after the floods.

Not everyone cares about rivers or fish. Most of the time, people don't see a strong connection between healthy landscapes and healthy communities. But after the floods of 1996, some understood the consequences of not learning how to live with rivers. A variety of county, state, and federal agencies began a reexamination of their policies to see where they could make improvements in relation to rivers, floods, and landslides. The Oregon Department of Forestry started a review of their forest practices regulations. The U.S. Forest Service would rely on findings by the H.J. Andrews scientists and other researchers about how to improve their forest management.

Teachers refer to "a teachable moment" when the student is open to learning new things. The floods had created a teachable moment when people might be willing to learn about the connection between watershed health and healthy communities. Biologist Jim Karr talked about taking responsibility for what we do:

As a society, we've spent a lot of money and energy protecting human health and economic health, but very little on ecological health. We've behaved as if our actions cause no ecological risk.

We have to understand the human health consequences and eco-logical health consequences of our actions.

Can we remember for the next thirty-two years?

A REGIONAL VISION

We need a regional vision for rivers and watersheds. We used to see rivers strictly as resources for production and systems to be engineered. We moved to seeing rivers as corridors—we cleaned up the sewage, designated some as national wild and scenic rivers, and established greenways along some stretches. Now we are beginning to see rivers as embedded in watersheds, with the development of watershed councils and watershed-level planning. We need to see the Pacific Northwest as a region of linked watersheds. We can rebuild regional watershed health the same way we would start work in a single watershed. Protect the healthy watersheds, secure them as strongholds for healthy rivers, and build outward, connecting healthy rivers to restored rivers.

We have some healthy watersheds. They are not completely healthy, but they have a high level of biological integrity. These watersheds can be the cornerstone of a regional restoration strategy. We have a lot of information about where to find these healthy watersheds.

The nonprofit organization Oregon Trout commissioned three biologists, including Willa Nehlsen, to develop a report on healthy salmon stocks in the Pacific Coast states. The biologists studied the same states as the "Crossroads" article: California, Oregon, Washington, and Idaho. They used a modest definition of healthy stocks—wild salmon runs had to be at least 10 percent as abundant as would be expected without human impacts, and abundant relative to available habitat. The stocks had to be stable; declining stocks did not qualify. Finally, no stocks were included that had been previously identified as being at risk.

The biologists found 121 healthy stocks of salmon and steelhead. Idaho had none; California had 1; Oregon had 46; and Washington had 74. The survey could be viewed as a report that the glass was half full, or one that the glass was half empty. The 121 healthy stocks were greatly outnumbered by the 214 stocks listed in the "Crossroads" study as at risk, and the 100 salmon runs listed as extinct. For California and Idaho, the glass was almost empty—the lack of healthy stocks in these two states showed how serious the salmon decline was. The report commented that the absence of healthy stocks in Idaho was "particularly troubling" because the state has a lot of high-quality salmon habitat. Unfortunately, there are a lot of dams between the habitat and the salmon.

The report was relatively good news for Oregon and Washington. These two states had substantial numbers of healthy stocks, a foundation for restoration. In Washington, the healthy salmon runs were clustered around the west coast of the Olympic Peninsula, upper Puget Sound, and the Wenatchee River and Hanford Reach in central Washington. Oregon's healthy salmon runs were grouped around the north coast from Tillamook to Astoria; the south coast, particularly the Umpqua River; and the John Day River. Both states had some healthy runs in other areas outside the main clusters.

The report pointed out that the healthy salmon runs were not secure. In the professional judgment of fish biologists familiar with the various runs, over 95 percent of the stocks were threatened by habitat degradation. Most of the region's restoration money was being spent on threatened and endangered or at-risk salmon. Although threatened stocks needed help, the report emphasized that it was vital to pay attention to the healthy stocks, and to protect their at-risk freshwater habitat before these stocks declined too. The healthy salmon runs were critical to maintaining the region's salmon.

The Forest Service and Bureau of Land Management manage millions of acres of publicly owned lands in the Pacific Northwest. The federal lands include the headwaters of many watersheds, and they also have the largest islands of the remaining healthiest watersheds.

For decades, the federal forest and range lands were managed under a multiple-use policy. Although recreation was important and some land was protected as wilderness, logging and grazing were also major uses. Logging was intensive on many federal forests during the last several decades. The agencies were accused of degrading other resources while "getting the cut out." By the early 1990s, lawsuits and court injunctions had stopped all logging on federal lands in the range of the spotted owl, which included western Washington, western Oregon, and northern California.

President Clinton stepped into the heated, gridlocked controversy shortly after he was elected in 1992. In the Clinton Forest Conference in Portland on April 2, 1993, he directed the federal agencies to develop a new plan for managing federal forests in the range of the spotted owl. The new plan was required to balance sustainable timber harvest with a new management approach that protected all species. The lawsuits had been brought over the spotted owl, but since then the first salmon stocks had been listed as threatened and endangered and the "Crossroads" article had been published. The status of fish and other aquatic species was a significant issue in the plan.

The planning group was called the Forest Ecosystem Management Assessment Team, or FEMAT. Gordon Reeves and Jim Sedell were the leaders of the aquatic group, charged to develop an aquatic conservation strategy for the federal forests. The two scientists had helped to develop the new understanding of river ecosystems. Now they had a chance to apply science to the management of large areas of federal forest land: 8,839,100 acres in western Washington and the Washington Cascades, and 9,564,100 acres in western Oregon and the Oregon Cascades.

The FEMAT Report was issued in 1993, and the Clinton Forest Plan in 1994. The plan was upheld through several legal challenges and, as of early 1997, is the management direction for Pacific Northwest federal forest lands from the Cascades to the Pacific Ocean.

The plan established key watersheds as the cornerstone of aquatic conservation on federal lands. The key watersheds contained vital habitat for salmon at risk, bull trout, and other resident fish species, or were primary sources of high-quality water. These watersheds would be a regional system of refugia and the anchor for recovering watersheds. They included some degraded habitat, and the plan directed that these areas should receive high priority for restoration work.

Lawsuits had forced the federal agencies to the table. But once there, they came up with a dramatic change in management direction that incorporated the newest scientific ideas on ecosystems and conservation. The agencies started to carry out the Clinton Forest Plan and in 1994 began a similar planning effort for federal lands in the interior of the Pacific Northwest.

The Interior Columbia Basin Ecosystem Management Project (ICBEMP) covered all federal forest lands and rangelands managed by the Forest Service and Bureau of Land Management in the interior Columbia River basin. The planning area included Oregon and Washington east of the Cascades, Idaho, and small parts of Montana, Wyoming, and Nevada.

Sources for map opposite: Based on maps from *Viability Assessments and Management Considerations for Species Associated with Late-Successional and Old-Growth Forests of the Pacific Northwest: The Report of the Scientific Analysis Team,* by Jack Ward Thomas et al., USDA Forest Service Research, 1993, and *Management History of Eastside Ecosystems: Change in Fish Habitat Over Fifty Years, 1935 to 1992,* by Bruce A. McIntosh et al, USDA Forest Service Pacific Northwest Research Station, 1994.

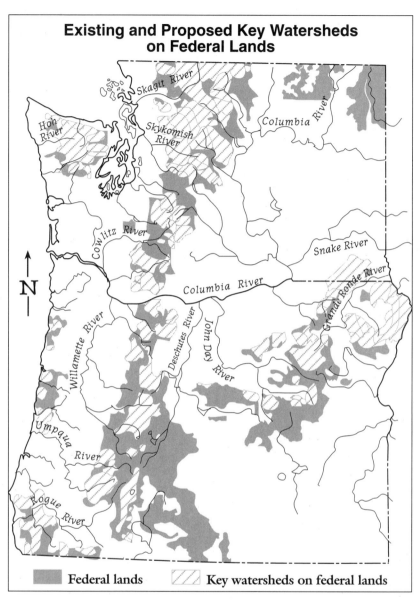

Existing and Proposed Key Watersheds on Federal Lands

Skagit River

Hoh River

Skykomish River

Columbia River

Cowlitz River

Snake River

N

Columbia River

Grande Ronde River

Willamette River

Deschutes River

John Day River

Umpqua River

Rogue River

Federal lands   **Key watersheds on federal lands**

The Clinton Forest Plan designated key watersheds on federal lands in western Oregon and Washington, and northern California. Key watersheds contain vital habitat for salmon and trout, or they are sources of high quality water. A 1994 scientific report on eastside fish habitat proposed key watersheds for federal lands in eastern Oregon and Washington. Key watersheds, along with wilderness areas and national parks, could be the foundation for a regional system of refugia for river ecosystems.

As of early 1997, the ICBEMP project had not yet proposed key watersheds. Forest Service scientists had prepared a report in 1994 that assessed changes in fish habitat in eastern Oregon and Washington over the last fifty years. This report recommended key watersheds for national forests in eastern Oregon and Washington, using criteria similar to the ones used in the Clinton Forest Plan. The report suggested that these key watersheds would serve as cornerstones for regional protection and restoration of aquatic ecosystems in eastern Oregon and Washington.

The list of designated and proposed key watersheds for Washington and Oregon reads like a list of the region's most famous rivers: Klamath, Illinois, Rogue, Elk, Coquille, Umpqua, Siuslaw, Willamette, McKenzie, Santiam, Clackamas, Cowlitz, Chehalis, Quinault, Elwha, Snoqualmie, Snohomish, Skykomish, Stillaguamish, Skagit, Nooksack, Methow, Wenatchee, Yakima, White Salmon, Walla Walla, Grande Ronde, John Day, and Deschutes. (The reports provide a more detailed listing; in most cases, various sub-basins of these watersheds are listed as the actual key watersheds.) The key watersheds include only federal lands.

As federal agencies, the Forest Service and Bureau of Land Management have a unique position in the region. They can manage their lands under a common policy and with a regional perspective, something not possible with private lands. The key watersheds could be the cornerstone of a regional restoration strategy for healthy rivers and watersheds, and the core of a regional system of refugia. But the federal lands alone cannot recover salmon or restore healthy rivers.

Restoration will have to reconnect rivers and habitats throughout watersheds. Private landowners, communities, and government agencies will need to cooperate and work together. We don't need to give up Western civilization. But we do need to articulate a regional vision that makes room for rivers as well as Western civilization.

Gordon Reeves explained the limitation of the key watersheds:

We are fighting a battle with one arm tied behind our backs because we are dealing only with federal lands. [We] designed the federal lands aquatic conservation strategy with the perception that little or nothing would be done on private lands. Historically, fish production was in the lower parts of the systems, not higher up. Fish need the full range of habitats.

We're not going back to natural systems. We shouldn't shoot for it. We pushed the streams to a domain not at all like the

natural domain, but we need to push them back toward the natu-
ral domain. We need to restore the essential processes.

Jim Karr emphasized how necessary it is that we reconcile people
and nature:

The success of human society has come from us understanding the
balance between our individual rights and community respon-
sibilities. The actions we take as individuals cascade across land-
scapes. We should limit our actions that have negative effects on
landscapes. Human rights are not ultimate. Without environ-
mental rights, human rights cannot exist.

STRONGHOLDS

Rivers never break. Our rivers have survived ice ages and volcanic eruptions.
They have been buried by lava flows and ice sheets. The Columbia River
has been dammed many times before in its millions of years. Do we really
think we can dam the river permanently, when volcanoes and ice ages were
only able to dam it for a little while?

Stan Gregory warned, "The human system is much more at risk than
the ecosystem. They'll be around after we go extinct."

Extinct salmon stocks cannot be brought back. But salmon have created new stocks before. Most of the Pacific Northwest salmon stocks have
evolved since the end of the last ice age. We don't know how long it takes
salmon to create a new stock. In New Zealand, where Pacific Northwest
chinook were transplanted at the beginning of the twentieth century, the
salmon are starting to show specific adaptations to the New Zealand rivers
through life history changes after seventy-five to eighty years in their new
environment. In Alaska, where glaciers are melting out of some rivers
right now, the salmon are there in a few years. But they come from nearby
rivers and similar habitats.

We are not seeing salmon recolonize rivers or develop new stocks in
the Pacific Northwest rivers. Jim Lichatowich pointed out that this is a
sign of the magnitude and persistence of the changes we have made to
our rivers. It is also the result of our inability to cut back on harvest and
too much reliance on hatcheries.

"It may take as long as a thousand years," said Chris Frissell. "What
we are trying to do with salmon is to save possibilities for restoration in
the lifespan of a human being, or in a few generations."

In the Pacific Northwest, all the rivers are missing at least some pieces. The best we have are the almost pristine rivers, the healthy salmon stocks, the key watersheds. The connections that should bind the pieces together in a resilient web are severed or frayed. But the Pacific Northwest rivers have more pieces than the rivers in the rest of the country. They have enough pieces that healing is possible.

The damage to river ecosystems was done over two centuries and cannot be quickly repaired. If we heal the landscape, rivers will heal themselves.

As Western civilization has rediscovered the sacred in nature, we have turned to the mountains. We have sought out rugged, remote, beautiful places and made them our wildernesses and national parks. But perhaps we should also turn to the low places where water runs and consider our rivers as sacred places. The rivers tell the story of everything we do. If we are good stewards of the land, the river will show it through clean water, cutthroat trout, returning salmon, osprey, great blue herons, and sleek otters catching fish.

We should say a prayer for all that the river still has. We should remember the fragility of refuge and the toughness of rivers.

Bibliographic Notes

Many people are working on river ecology issues, and there is a wealth of information available. Some of the key references I used are discussed below. Any one of them will lead the reader on to many other sources.

Government reports may still be available directly from the agency itself if they are recent. Older reports can be found in the libraries of large universities such as the University of Oregon, which maintains an entire room of government documents. Scientific journals can be found in university libraries. Often local public libraries can get articles from these journals through interlibrary loan programs for reasonable fees. Many articles can be found through electronic databases, but know what fees you're incurring before you order. Some electronic databases charge reasonable fees; others are very expensive.

The Internet World Wide Web sites listed below have information about rivers in the Pacific Northwest as well as other resource issues.

H.J. Andrews Experimental Forest   http://www.fsl.orst.edu/lter
U.S. Forest Service   http://www.fs.fed.us/
U.S. Forest Service and Bureau of Land Management, Interior Columbia Basin
      Ecosystem Management Project   http://www.icbemp.gov
National Marine Fisheries Service, list of links to Pacific salmon information
      http://kingfish.ssp.nmfs.gov/salmon/salmon.html
High Country News   http://www.hcn.org

The *High Country News* is a biweekly newspaper that covers natural resource issues and news throughout the western states (except California). For subscription information, visit their Web site or write Box 1090, Paonia, CO 81428.

Prologue

For basic information about the winter of 1995–96 and the floods of '96, I relied on local newspapers, including the Eugene *Register-Guard* and the Portland *Oregonian,* local television news programs, and Associated

Press reports posted on CompuServe, an electronic information service (to find out how to subscribe to CompuServe, go to their Internet World Wide Web site at: http://www.compuserve.com). For regional effects on federal lands, see *Storms and Floods of the Winter of 1995–1996: An Assessment of Effects on USDA Forest Service and USDI Bureau of Land Management Lands* (Portland: USDA Forest Service, Pacific Northwest Region, Natural Resources, May 22, 1996). Flood effects on the Willamette National Forest and the Willamette River are summarized in *Willamette National Forest Flood Narrative: The Great Flood of 1996* (Eugene, Ore.: USDA Forest Service, Willamette National Forest, 1996). For flood effects on forest lands in general, see *Aerial Reconnaissance Evaluation of 1996 Storm Effects on Upland Mountainous Watersheds of Oregon and Southern Washington,* by Pacific Watershed Associates (survey done in February/March 1996 for the Pacific Rivers Council; report available from Pacific Rivers Council, P.O. Box 10798, Eugene, OR 97440).

Chapter 1

For regional geographical information and statistics, my basic sources were *Atlas of the Pacific Northwest,* edited by Philip L. Jackson and A. Jon Kimerling (Corvallis: Oregon State University Press, 1993) and standard atlases. For statistics on the Columbia River basin, dams in the Pacific Northwest, and salmon run declines, I used mainly federal government documents, including *The Columbia River System: The Inside Story,* by Bonneville Power Administration et al. (System Operation Review Interagency Team, P.O. Box 2988, Portland, OR 97208-2988, document number DOE/BP-1689, 1994). *The Inside Story* was published as part of a comprehensive system operation review for the Columbia River dams; many other documents were published and may still be available. Other federal agency documents on the Columbia I used were *Strategy for Salmon,* vols. 1 and 2, by Northwest Power Planning Council (851 SW Sixth Avenue, Suite 1100, Portland, OR 97204, document numbers 92-21 and 92-21A, 1992).

The nonprofit organization Pacific Rivers Council (PRC) has many excellent publications about Pacific Northwest rivers and restoration strategies and also gives workshops on river restoration. For information on their publications, workshops, and membership, write Pacific Rivers Council, P.O. Box 10798, Eugene, OR 97440. Their *Entering the Watershed: A New Approach to Save America's River Ecosystems,* by Bob Doppelt, Mary Scurlock, Chris Frissell, and James Karr (Washington,

D.C.: Island Press, 1993) gives a good overview of watershed health and restoration. River conservation groups and community colleges in your area may also give workshops related to river ecology and conservation.

Chapter 2

I found *A View of the River,* by Luna B. Leopold (Cambridge: Harvard University Press, 1994) to be an excellent introduction to the principles of river hydrology. The best single source on the principles of river ecology is *Watershed Management: Balancing Sustainability and Environmental Change,* edited by Robert J. Naiman (proceedings of the symposium "New Perspectives for Watershed Management in the Pacific Northwest," held in Seattle November 27–29, 1990; New York: Springer-Verlag, 1992). Springer-Verlag is also publishing, in 1997, a new book edited by Robert J. Naiman and Robert E. Bilby, *The Ecology and Management of Streams and Rivers in the Pacific Coastal Ecoregion,* which will report on new research since the symposium.

A good book on the importance of wood in river ecosystems is *From the Forest to the Sea: The Ecology of Wood in Streams, Rivers, Estuaries, and Oceans,* by Chris Maser and James R. Sedell (Delray Beach, Fla.: St. Lucie Press, 1994). Two key research papers are "The River Continuum Concept," by R. L. Vannote, G. W. Minshall, K. W. Cummins, J. R. Sedell, and C. E. Cushing (*Canadian Journal of Fisheries and Aquatic Sciences* 37:130–137, 1980) and "An Ecosystem Perspective of Riparian Zones," by Stanley V. Gregory, Frederick J. Swanson, W. Arthur McKee, and Kenneth W. Cummins (*BioScience* 41[8]: 540–551, 1991). All of these books and articles have long lists of references to additional work on these subjects.

Chapter 3

Geological information is from *After the Ice Age: The Return of Life to Glaciated North America,* by E. C. Pielou (Chicago: University of Chicago Press, 1991) and from David D. Alt and Donald W. Hyndman's *Roadside Geology of Oregon* (Missoula, Mont.: Mountain Press, 1981) and *Roadside Geology of Washington* (Mountain Press, 1984).

The assessment of the Chiwawa River after the 1990 flood is from *Management History of Eastside Ecosystems: Changes in Fish Habitat Over 50 Years, 1935 to 1992,* by Bruce A. McIntosh et al. (Portland, Ore.: USDA Forest Service, Pacific Northwest Research Station, General Technical Report PNW-GTR-321, February 1994). This publication also has detailed information on several other watersheds east of the Cascades. The

Pacific Northwest Research Station (PNW), is part of the Forest Service's research branch, which conducts scientific research independently from the national forest system. PNW's scientists have produced many outstanding publications, which can be ordered by calling 503-326-7128, or by writing to USDA Forest Service, PNW, P.O. Box 3890, Portland, OR 97208.

For more information on disturbances and dynamics in rivers, see *A View of the River* and *Watershed Management,* discussed under the bibliographic notes for Chapter 2, and also *The Ecology of Natural Disturbance and Patch Dynamics,* by S. T. A. Pickett and P. S. White (New York: Academic Press, 1985). Just two of the many research papers on disturbance and recovery are "Overview of Case Studies on Recovery of Aquatic Systems from Disturbance," by Gerald J. Niemi et al. (*Environmental Management* 14[5]: 571–587, 1990) and "Patch Dynamics in Lotic Systems: The Stream as a Mosaic," by C. M. Pringle et al. (*Journal of the North American Benthological Society* 7: 503–524, 1988).

Salmon survival strategies are described in many places, but one of the most useful summaries is in *Wild Salmon Forever: A Citizens' Strategy to Restore Northwest Salmon and Watersheds* (Save Our Wild Salmon Coalition, 1516 Melrose Avenue, Suite 200, Seattle, WA 98122, 1994). Several of the scientists I interviewed contributed to this report. My sentence "Life meets change and surprise with resilience" is based on remarks in *Compass and Gyroscope,* by Kai N. Lee (Washington, D.C.: Island Press, 1993).

Chapter 4

For the history of rivers in the Pacific Northwest, I relied on many standard historical sources, which were also references for Chapters 5–8. These books include *The Pacific Northwest: An Interpretive History,* by Carlos A. Schwantes (Lincoln: University of Nebraska Press, 1989); standard histories of Oregon, Washington, and Idaho; and for Indian management of salmon fishing, *Nch'i-Wana "The Big River": Mid-Columbia Indians and Their Land,* by Eugene S. Hunn, with James Selam and family (Seattle: University of Washington Press, 1990). *From the Forest to the Sea* (see bibliographic notes for Chapter 2) has information on snagging and channelizing the Willamette and other rivers in the 1800s.

For the Columbia River, a standard history is *The Columbia,* by Stewart Holbrook (New York: Holt, Rinehart, and Winston, 1956). I particularly recommend *The Organic Machine: The Remaking of the Columbia River,* by Richard White (New York: Hill and Wang/Farrar, Strauss, &

Giroux, 1995), especially for its insightful interpretation. For the classic history of what happened to the Columbia River salmon runs in the nineteenth and twentieth centuries, read *The Columbia River Salmon and Steelhead Trout: Their Fight for Survival,* by Anthony Netboy (Seattle: University of Washington Press, 1980).

For the history of rivers in eastern Oregon and Washington, see also *A History of Resource Use and Disturbance in Riverine Basins of Eastern Oregon and Washington (Early 1800s–1990s),* by Robert C. Wissmar et al. (*Northwest Science* 68 [special issue], 1994). Also see *Management History of Eastside Ecosystems* under bibliographic notes for Chapter 3.

Chapter 5

For the Elwha River and other Olympic Peninsula rivers and their salmon, the classic work is *Mountain in the Clouds: A Search for the Wild Salmon,* by Bruce Brown (New York: Collier Books/Macmillan, 1982, 1990). The National Park Service has published a number of documents on the Elwha and the proposal to remove the two dams. The initial report, which includes history and description of the river, is *The Elwha Report: Restoration of the Elwha River Ecosystem & Native Anadromous Fisheries* (Washington, D.C.: U.S. Department of the Interior, January 1994).

For the history of dams on the Willamette River, see *The Return of a River: The Willamette River, Oregon,* by George W. Gleeson (Corvallis: Oregon State University, June 1972) and also *The Willamette Valley Project of Oregon,* by William G. Robbins (*Pacific Historical Review* 47: 585–605, 1978).

For the history and effects of dams on the Columbia River, see *The Inside Story* and other System Operation Review documents, and *Strategy for Salmon* (both discussed under bibliographic notes for Chapter 1). The hydrograph of the Columbia referred to at the end of Chapter 5 is in *The Inside Story.*

The ecological effects of dams are discussed in *Watershed Management* (see bibliographic notes for Chapter 2); in *Entering the Watershed* (see notes for Chapter 1); and also in "Downstream Ecological Effects of Dams," by Franklin K. Ligon et al. (*BioScience* 45[3]: 183–92, 1995). For information on the contributions of salmon carcasses in streams, see "Fate of Coho Salmon *(Oncorhynchus kisutch)* Carcasses in Spawning Streams," by C. J. Cederholm et al. (*Canadian Journal of Fisheries and Aquatic Sciences* 46: 1347–1355, 1989) and "Role of Coho Salmon Carcasses in Maintaining Stream Productivity: Evidence from Nitrogen and Carbon Stable Isotopes," by Robert E. Bilby et al. (in *Salmon*

Ecosystem Restoration: Myth and Reality, edited by Mary Louise Keefe; proceedings of the 1994 Northeast Pacific Chinook and Coho Salmon Workshop, Eugene, Ore., November 7–10, 1994. For copies send $15 to Oregon Chapter, American Fisheries Society, P.O. Box 722, Corvallis, OR 97339.)

The two classic books on water development and irrigation in the American West are *Cadillac Desert*, by Marc Reisner (New York: Viking Penguin, 1986) and *Rivers of Empire: Water, Aridity, and the Growth of the American West*, by Donald Worster (New York: Pantheon, 1985).

Chapter 6

For information on the John Day River basin, see the publications for river history in eastern Oregon discussed in the Chapter 4 bibliographic notes. For information about The Nature Conservancy preserves in Oregon, contact The Nature Conservancy, 821 SE 14th Avenue, Portland, OR 97214. Information on the effects of forest practices on rivers can be found in *Watershed Management* (see Chapter 2 bibliographic notes) and also *Cumulative Effects of Forest Practices in Oregon: Executive Summary*, by Stanley V. Gregory et al. (report prepared by authors at Oregon State University, Corvallis, for the Oregon Department of Forestry, Salem, Ore., March 1995).

One of the most influential publications on the effects of forest practices on rivers is *Forest Ecosystem Management: An Ecological, Economic, and Social Assessment: Report of the Forest Ecosystem Management Assessment Team* (Portland, Ore.: USDA Forest Service, Pacific Northwest Region, 1993). The report is known by Forest Service employees simply as FEMAT. The study that documented the loss of pools in rivers is *Historic Changes in Pool Habitat for Columbia River Basin Salmon Under Study for TES Listing*, by James R. Sedell and Fred H. Everest (Corvallis, Ore.: USDA Forest Service, Pacific Northwest Research Station, 1991).

Various research articles will eventually be published on the effects of the flood of 1996 on streams in the H.J. Andrews Experimental Forest. Right now, the best source for information on flood effects is the H.J. Andrews Web site, listed at the beginning of these notes.

Chapter 7

The cleanup of the Willamette River is described in *The Return of a River* (see Chapter 5 bibliographic notes). Information on contaminants in the lower Columbia River is from *The Health of the River 1990–1996:*

Integrated Technical Report, by Tetra Tech, Inc. (prepared for the Lower Columbia River Bi-State Water Quality Program, 1996). The document has a list of the additional reports generated by the research program, and of new studies that are under way. Contact the Washington Department of Ecology, Publications Distribution, P.O. Box 47600, Olympia, WA 98504-7600; phone 360-407-7472. I relied on newspaper articles in the *Oregonian* and *Register-Guard* for additional information on contaminant studies.

For the history of Hanford Nuclear Reservation, the best single source is *On the Home Front: The Cold War Legacy of the Hanford Nuclear Site*, by Michele Stenehjen Gerber (Lincoln: University of Nebraska Press, 1992). See also *Closing the Circle on the Splitting of the Atom: The Environmental Legacy of Nuclear Weapons Production in the United States and What the Department of Energy Is Doing About It* (Office of Environmental Management, U.S. Department of Energy, 1000 Independence Avenue SW, Washington, DC 20585, January 1995).

Chapter 8

The seminal article on the Pacific Northwest salmon crisis is "Pacific Salmon at the Crossroads: Stocks at Risk from California, Oregon, Idaho, and Washington," by Willa Nehlsen, Jack E. Williams, and James A. Lichatowich (*Fisheries* 16[2]: 4–21, 1991). For a history of the growing regional awareness of the salmon crisis, read *A Common Fate: Endangered Salmon and the People of the Pacific Northwest*, by Joseph Cone (New York: Henry Holt, 1995).

For the relationship between ocean conditions, freshwater habitat, and salmon, see "Cycles in Ocean Productivity, Trends in Habitat Quality, and the Restoration of Salmon Runs in Oregon," by Peter W. Lawson (*Fisheries* 18[8]: 6–10, 1983).

Additional information on the decline of salmon can be found in *Status and Future of Salmon of Western Oregon and Northern California: Overview of Findings and Options*, by Daniel B. Botkin et al. (Center for the Study of the Environment, P.O. Box 6945, Santa Barbara, CA 93160; research report 951002, 1995). For information on the status of all Pacific Coast fish, see "Topology of Decline and Extinction of Fishes in the Pacific Northwest and California, U.S.A.," by Christopher A. Frissell (*Conservation Biology* 7[2]: 342–354, 1993). The decline of mollusks is discussed in *Mollusc Species of Special Concern Within the Range of the Northern Spotted Owl*, by Terrence J. Frest and Edward J. Johannes (report prepared for the FEMAT Working Group, USDA Forest Service,

Portland, Ore., by Deixis Consultants, 2517 NE 65th Street, Seattle, WA 98115-7125, 1993).

Information on the Index of Biotic Integrity (IBI) is available in many articles. Good introductions are "Biological Integrity Versus Biological Diversity as Policy Directives: Protecting Biotic Resources," by Paul L. Angermeier and James R. Karr (*BioScience* 44[10], 1994); "Clean Water Is Not Enough," by James R. Karr (*illahee* 11[1–2]: 51–59, 1995); and finally, "Biological Integrity: A Long-Neglected Aspect of Water Resource Management," by James R. Karr (*Ecological Applications* 1: 66–84, 1991).

Chapter 9

For my discussion of restoration principles, I relied on several publications by Pacific Rivers Council, including *Entering the Watershed* (see bibliographic notes for Chapter 1) and *Wild Salmon Forever,* by Save Our Wild Salmon Coalition (see Chapter 3 bibliographic notes). Other information came from various workshops and conferences, where I benefited from the ideas of many people who know far more about restoration than I do. For the inspiring story of kids who adopted an urban stream in Everett, Washington, and brought it back to life, read *Come Back, Salmon,* by Molly Cone, with photographs by Sidnee Wheelwright (San Francisco: Sierra Club Books for Children, 1992).

To get involved in restoration, seek out your local watershed council or river conservation group. Two excellent regional/national organizations are Pacific Rivers Council (see Chapter 1 bibliographic notes for address) and River Network, P.O. Box 8787, Portland, OR 97207. Both organizations can help you find out if your area has a local group working on river issues (or help you start a local group). The leading national river conservation organization is American Rivers, 1025 Vermont Avenue NW, Suite 720, Washington, DC 20005. Federal and state land management agencies and fishery management agencies all include some type of public involvement in their planning processes, such as public meetings, hearings, or comment periods.

For the comparison of cost-effectiveness in restoration projects, see "Restoration of Habitat-Forming Processes in Pacific Northwest Watersheds: A Locally Adaptable Approach to Salmonid Habitat Restoration," by Tim Beechie, Eric Beamer, Brian Collins, and Lee Benda (in *The Role of Restoration in Ecosystem Management,* edited by David L. Pearson and Charles V. Klimas [Society for Ecological Restoration, 1207 Seminole Highway, Madison, WI 53711, 1996]; proceedings of symposium held by the Society for Ecological Restoration, in Seattle, Wash., September 14–16, 1995.)

Chapter 10

For designated key watersheds on federal lands in western Oregon and Washington, see the Clinton Forest Plan, formally known as *Final Supplemental Environmental Impact Statement on Management of Habitat for Late-Successional and Old-Growth Forest Related Species Within the Range of the Northern Spotted Owl* (Portland, Ore.: USDA Forest Service, Pacific Northwest Region, 1994). Also see the SAT Report (its full name is *Viability Assessments and Management Considerations for Species Associated with Late-Successional and Old-Growth Forests of the Pacific Northwest: The Report of the Scientific Analysis Team*), by Jack Ward Thomas et al. (Portland, Ore.: USDA Forest Service, March 1993). Proposals are still being developed for key watersheds on federal land in eastern Oregon and Washington, and in Idaho. Contact the Interior Columbia Basin Ecosystem Management Project (ICBEMP), 112 E. Poplar Street, Walla Walla, WA 99362, for their free newsletter, *The Leading Edge,* and information on publications available. Two ICBEMP-related reports are *Management History of Eastside Ecosystems* (see bibliographic notes for Chapter 3) and *Overview and Executive Summary: Status of the Interior Columbia Basin: Summary of Scientific Findings* (Portland, Ore.: USDA Forest Service and USDI Bureau of Land Management, General Technical Report PNW-GTR-385, 1996). I used the key watersheds maps from the SAT Report and *Management History of Eastside Ecosystems* for the key watersheds map in Chapter 10.

For more information on how to design a system of refugia for aquatic ecosystems, see "Role of Refugia in Recovery from Disturbances: Modern Fragmented and Disconnected River Systems," by J. R. Sedell et al. (*Environmental Management* 14: 711–724, 1990). Also see *Battle Against Extinction: Native Fish Management in the American West,* edited by W. L. Minckley and J. E. Deacon (Tucson: University of Arizona Press, 1991). For information on healthy salmon stocks, see *Healthy Native Stocks of Anadromous Salmonids in the Pacific Northwest and California,* by Charles W. Huntington et al. (prepared for Oregon Trout, 5331 SW Macadam, Suite 228, Portland, OR 97201, December 31, 1994).

For a good discussion of water policy in western states and suggestions for reform, see *Searching Out the Headwaters: Change and Rediscovery in Western Water Policy,* by Sarah F. Bates et al. (Washington, D.C.: Island Press, 1993).

Index

U

U.S. Army Corps of Engineers 79, 94
U.S. Forest Service
  and flood of '96 121
  and key watersheds 166
  and land management 183
  and river restoration 161
  and scientific research 42
  and watershed approach 33
Umatilla River 78, 113
Umpqua River 15, 25
Upper Klamath Lake 114–115

W

Wahluke Slope 134, 139, 140
Washington Public Power Supply System (WPPSS) 139
water rights 113–114, 174
Water temperatures 102–103
Watershed councils 171
watershed restoration, principles of 176
watersheds
  and connections to rivers 26, 31
  and broken connections to rivers 32
  definition of 24
  and ecological patterns 48–49
  and land use practices 112
Wenatchee River 61
Wenatchee River Salmon Festival 143
Wenatchee, Lake 59
Willamette Mission State Park 86
Willamette River
  and flood of '96 13
  and salmon runs 71
  and toxic chemicals 132–133
  cleanup of 126–127
  dams and flood control 96–97
  flood of record 178
  floodplain restoration 173
  greenway 127
  historical removal of snags 79
  in the 1800s 27
  in the 1960s 28
  modern 84–86
  pollution of 93
  water quality of 94
Willamette Valley, and the flood of '96 122
Williams, Jack 143
Williamson River 114
Wilson River 180–181

Y

Yakima River 113

About the Author

A natural resource writer and writing consultant, Valerie Rapp is the winner of a 1996 fellowship in nonfiction from Literary Arts, Inc in Oregon. In addition to *What the River Reveals*, her recent writing projects have included two books for middle school grades, one on the Pacific Northwest old growth forests and the second on the Columbia River basin ecosystem and its wild salmon. Val has worked in natural resource management since 1978, and, in addition to writing forest management and habitat conservation plans, she has had jobs in wildland firefighting, helicopter rappelling, trail work, timber sale planning, and wild and scenic river planning. She has a B.A. in English literature from the State University of New York at Buffalo. She lives with her husband, Gene Skrine, in the McKenzie River Valley, Oregon. Three stepchildren are also an important part of her family.

THE MOUNTAINEERS, founded in 1906, is a nonprofit outdoor activity and conservation club, whose mission is "to explore, study, preserve, and enjoy the natural beauty of the outdoors. . . ." Based in Seattle, Washington, the club is now the third-largest such organization in the United States, with 15,000 members and five branches throughout Washington State.

The Mountaineers sponsors both classes and year-round outdoor activities in the Pacific Northwest, which include hiking, mountain climbing, ski-touring, snowshoeing, bicycling, camping, kayaking and canoeing, nature study, sailing, and adventure travel. The club's conservation division supports environmental causes through educational activities, sponsoring legislation, and presenting informational programs. All club activities are led by skilled, experienced volunteers, who are dedicated to promoting safe and responsible enjoyment and preservation of the outdoors.

If you would like to participate in these organized outdoor activities or the club's programs, consider a membership in The Mountaineers. For information and an application, write or call The Mountaineers, Club Headquarters, 300 Third Avenue West, Seattle, Washington 98119; (206) 284-6310.

The Mountaineers Books, an active, nonprofit publishing program of the club, produces guidebooks, instructional texts, historical works, natural history guides, and works on environmental conservation. All books produced by The Mountaineers are aimed at fulfilling the club's mission.

Send or call for our catalog of more than 300 outdoor titles:

The Mountaineers Books
1001 SW Klickitat Way, Suite 201
Seattle, WA 98134
1-800-553-4453 / e-mail: mbooks@mountaineers.org

Other titles you may enjoy from Mountaineers Books:

THE COLUMBIA:
SUSTAINING A MODERN RESOURCE, Palmer
Large format, full-color pictorial celebrates the landscape and people that shape this great American river, offering solid solutions for its sustainability.

SOCKEYE SALMON:
A PICTORIAL TRIBUTE, Naito & Paine
Spectacular portfolio of over 70 full-color photographs depicts the mysterious and fascinating life cycle of the sockeye salmon.

THE PRICE OF TAMING A RIVER:
THE DECLINE OF PUGET SOUND'S DUWAMISH/GREEN WATERWAY, Sato
Portrait of a fragile waterway destroyed by agriculture and industry, and the inspirational stories of the people attempting to protect and preserve it.

DEAD RECKONING:
CONFRONTING THE CRISIS IN PACIFIC FISHERIES, Glavin
Thoroughly researched, in-depth account of the West Coast's dwindling fish populations and the perilous state of the Pacific fisheries. Offers solutions to ensure long-term sustainability.

NISQUALLY WATERSHED:
GLACIER TO DELTA, A RIVER'S LEGACY, Gordon & Lembersky
70 color photographs and text profile this model watershed.

A TIDEWATER PLACE:
PORTRAIT OF THE WILLAPA ECOSYSTEM, Wolf
Human and natural history of the Willapa Bay area of southwest Washington. Published by the Willapa Alliance with the Nature Conservancy and Ecotrust.

WASHINGTON'S WILD RIVERS:
THE UNFINISHED WORK, McNulty & O'Hara
Prose and full-color photographs explain Northwest rivers, and existing systems for protecting them.